# TEAC

## REBOOTED

# OTHER TITLES BY JON TAIT

*100 Ideas for Secondary Teachers: Engaging Learners*

*Bloomsbury CPD Library: Senior Leadership*

*Succeeding as a Head of Year*

# Using the science of learning to transform classroom practice

**Jon Tait**

BLOOMSBURY EDUCATION

LONDON   OXFORD   NEW YORK   NEW DELHI   SYDNEY

BLOOMSBURY EDUCATION
Bloomsbury Publishing Plc
50 Bedford Square, London, WC1B 3DP, UK
29 Earlsfort Terrace, Dublin 2, Ireland

BLOOMSBURY, BLOOMSBURY EDUCATION and the Diana logo are trademarks of
Bloomsbury Publishing Plc

First published in Great Britain, 2020

A catalogue record for this book is available from the British Library

ISBN: PB: 978-1-4729-7766-3; ePDF: 978-1-4729-7769-4; ePub: 978-1-4729-7767-0

4 6 8 10 9 7 5 3 (paperback)

Text design by Marcus Duck Design

Typeset by Newgen KnowledgeWorks Pvt. Ltd., Chennai, India
Printed and bound in the UK by CPI Group (UK) Ltd, Croydon, CR0 4YY

MIX
Paper from
responsible sources
FSC® C013604

To find out more about our authors and books visit www.bloomsbury.com
and sign up for our newsletters

# CONTENTS

# ACKNOWLEDGEMENTS

To the teachers, researchers and academics whom I have referenced in this book, thank you. I thank you for your countless and painstaking hours of laboratory testing, fieldwork and meta-analysis of thousands of educational studies from across the world.

To the academics whose research turned out to be too inaccessible to the average classroom teacher, the journalists who intentionally distorted and reported the research, and the teachers and school leaders who misinterpreted this research, I thank you all for giving me a reason to write.

To my publishing team, Bloomsbury, for continuing to believe in me as a credible voice on education and giving me a platform to write my fourth book. I will always be thankful for this opportunity to put my thoughts on paper and share them with teachers and school leaders all over the world.

And finally, to my own team at home – Team Tait. We laugh, we joke, we love and we listen. We make mistakes, we forgive, we hug and we support each other. Family is, and always will be, the most important thing. You inspire me every day to be the best husband and father that I can be.

Thank you x

# INTRODUCTION

So much teacher training and professional development over the last 20 years has been devoted to areas such as relationship building, behaviour management and the ability to engage students. It goes without saying that these are all vitally important skills, and without them you are certainly not going to be an effective teacher. However, there are some areas of professional knowledge and learning that appear to have been missing from almost everyone's professional toolkit. Among the most alarming are the very fundamentals about how we learn and retain information as human beings. When you strip back what our core business is as teachers, and how our students (whether we like it or not) are assessed at the end of our input to judge how well they have progressed under our care, it staggers me that, as a profession, we have not paid closer attention to the research on how students learn most efficiently and effectively. Far too much time has been spent thinking that, if we ensure our students are engaged (or, in some of the worst cases, 'entertained'), then they will somehow just 'get it' when the time comes to put pen to paper in the exam hall.

Engaging students is only half the battle. Getting students engaged in what you are delivering is paramount, but that still doesn't mean that they are going to remember everything you are talking about when they come to be assessed on it. The blood, sweat and tears that we lose at the front of our classroom every day may be completely wasted if we don't have a good grasp of cognitive science and the implications this may have on our classroom craft. From planning to assessing and everything in between, cognitive science should form the bedrock on which we stand as teachers. Unnecessary time, money and resources should not be wasted on strategies that have already been proven not to be particularly successful. Blindly trialling new approaches on students and using them as your crash-test dummies when there is already a wealth of research on what might be your best bets in the classroom is almost negligent as a professional.

Rest assured though, evidence-based teaching isn't about removing human judgement, experience and essential knowledge of context from the decision-making of teachers and replacing it with a raft of research reports and directives that teachers must follow in robotic form. Evidence and educational research should add to the experience and skill of a teacher to help their strategic decision-making, ensuring it becomes more reliable, efficient and effective. Robert Coe, Director of Research and Evaluation at Evidence Based Education, sums this up very well: 'Research can never tell teachers what to do, nor should it; it can, however, help provide teachers and leaders with what Prof. Steve Higgins (and others) have called "best bets". It can – and should – provide the theory underpinning the action in classrooms, leadership meetings, governing body committees and policy-making discussions.' (Coe and Kime, 2019)

# A MORE MEDICAL APPROACH TO TEACHING

One way of looking at the role of evidence in education is by comparing teaching with the medical profession. You wouldn't expect to go to the hospital and have a surgeon try out a new medical procedure on you, just because he or she thought it sounded like a good idea. However, there was a time when this was the norm. In his article 'Building Evidence into Education', Ben Goldacre (2013), a doctor and academic, explains that before evidence-based medicine made a more common and consistent appearance in hospitals and doctors' surgeries up and down the country, medical practice was driven by the personal experience of the doctor in front of you. Goldacre says: 'Many doctors – especially the most senior ones – fought hard against [evidence-based medicine], regarding [it] as a challenge to their authority. In retrospect, we've seen that these doctors were wrong. The opportunity to make informed decisions about what works best, using good-quality evidence, represents a truer form of professional independence than any senior figure barking out their opinions.'

Unfortunately, an identical situation has been happening in classrooms up and down the country for decades, with us teachers trying to find effective ways to get students to learn by a process of trial and error, with very little evidence to back up our choices and strategic decisions. In our defence, unlike the common cold or a broken leg, which can probably be treated as similarly in Middlesex as it can in Middlesbrough, context is key in education. No one child is the same and, as the experienced ones amongst us will tell you, even a strategy that works for a group of students before lunch might not be a successful strategy straight after lunch. Dylan Wiliam summed this up perfectly in 2015 when he said, 'in education, everything works somewhere and nothing works everywhere'. Having said that though, a set of guiding principles, firmly rooted in robust and globally accepted research, would be a great place to start when thinking about how we might teach our children. Irrespective of the specific context that a teacher may find themselves in, whether influenced by socio-economic or geographical factors or even gender bias, robust research from globally accepted studies can provide tried-and-tested theories that are based on biology and psychology – and not just on hearsay and rumour.

Thankfully, with a trend of research-informed practice sweeping into schools, a new dawn has broken across the educational landscape, shining light on how we truly learn as human beings. Research on cognitive science by leading academics from some of the finest universities across the world is now being brought into the mainstream education arena and teachers are beginning to use it as a basis for their classroom practice. Organisations such as the Education Endowment Foundation, Evidence Based Education, ResearchEd, The Chartered College of Teaching and the Research Schools Network, to name just a few, are making huge strides in this area. The emergence of this research into the mainstream classroom does carry its own problems (as we'll see on page xiii), but the very fact that teachers and school leaders are beginning to consult key pieces of international research on cognition, before they plan, write and deliver their curriculum, means that there is a definite shift happening. If we pride ourselves on delivering a world-class education system for our children, then surely we also need to pride ourselves on the fact that our strategies for getting the best out of those children are based on firm foundations, rather than a guessing game in the hope that something might work for the majority.

Having started my teaching career through the Graduate Teacher Programme (GTP), I wondered if I'd somehow missed out on this bedrock of educational research and knowledge. I felt I may have been one of the very few imposters in education, happily going about my business every day, without the knowledge of these studies underpinning my classroom practice. Luckily for me, but probably sadly for the profession and the children who have passed through our classrooms before us (and we can count ourselves in that), everyone I meet and talk to about this is coming to the same conclusion – it's time to stop the guessing games and begin acting on what we know works.

# ENGAGING WITH RESEARCH

In hindsight, teachers (including myself) have probably been given far too much freedom to think up their own strategies of how to get students to learn information and then perform well on their assessments and exams. This trial-and-error system has not only caused vital time to be wasted in the classroom, but it has undoubtedly put significant amounts of pressure on individual teachers to come up with 'the answer' to their professional conundrums. I am absolutely adamant that, if the research we are learning about now had been common knowledge between teachers 30 years ago when I started secondary school, many of the weird and wonderful strategies that we've seen or experienced during this time wouldn't have made it past the initial planning stage on the back of a beer mat. That's not to say I think we should have factory-like schools, where teachers are robbed of their creativity and children are all taught in the same way just because a study has recommended it. Far from it. Our children need creative teachers to light up their imagination and passion for their subject. Their creativity and energy just need to be channelled in different ways. Too much time is being spent trying to reinvent how the brain retains information, or planning tasks and resources that have no impact on learning. Engagement with research should not only improve the reliability of the strategic decisions you make in the classroom, but should also help to reduce your workload. You will inevitably spend less time thinking up strategies that may have little impact, and you will need to plan fewer intervention activities because your strategies will be more effective the first time round.

# SHARING RESEARCH WITH STUDENTS AND PARENTS

Research should not just be kept in the clutches of the teachers, like a secret code that stays within the magic circle. Passing on key messages to our students on the most efficient and effective ways to study should be one of our main priorities as teachers. If we can stop children making the same time-honoured mistakes as we made when we had to revise for our exams, by just re-reading our notes, and instead use some internationally recognised strategies on how to build effective study habits, then we might have just found a game changer. It is also key for our students to understand 'the why' behind our curriculum principles and why we have sequenced the curriculum like we have. Whether it is so they understand why you are spacing out their learning, or why you are quizzing them on a unit they studied a couple of months ago, it makes the 'desirable difficulties' that you are introducing into your classroom practice make sense to everyone.

There are also benefits of drip-feeding some of these key principles of how we learn to the parents and carers of our students. You can be sure that, if the teaching professionals haven't been aware of the research behind cognitive science and how we learn, the majority of parents won't have either. In my experience, the vast majority of parents really want to support their child at home, but sometimes feel unable to do so, due to a lack of significant subject knowledge needed under the new examination specifications. However, by educating parents on how their child can better understand and retain information (irrespective of the subject content), and the simple but effective role they can play in that, you can begin to maximise the impact of your actions as a school. Many of the guiding principles, once broken down into bite-sized chunks or headline messages, can easily be picked up by parents and implemented at home to support children to reach their true potential.

# THE PROBLEMS WITH RESEARCH

It is quite startling that some of the theories, strategies and practices that teachers have come to count on through folklore and staffroom whispers are at odds with what some of the research is now telling us (think learning styles or Brain Gym®). Even more surprising is that some of this research isn't hot off the press either. It is research that has been around since before many of us began our teaching careers and in some cases before we were even born. Take, for instance, Ebbinghaus's Forgetting Curve way back in

1885 (see page 15), Bjork's work on retrieval practice in 1975 (see page 3) or Sweller's cognitive load theory from 1988 (see page 92) All of these theories are fundamental to how we learn and we'll take a deeper look at them in the chapters of this book. If you're reading this book as a seasoned teacher or even as someone who has just passed their NQT year, you may be frustrated at how much time you could have saved yourself if you'd known about these theories in your training year – and, more importantly, how many children could have been exposed to better teaching techniques, meaning that they acquired more long-term knowledge and improved their life chances as a result.

So why has it taken this long for the profession to grab hold of evidence-based research, take it out of the clutches of the academics and put it in the hands of the teachers in our classrooms? And why, if some of the research has made it through the iron fences of our schools, has it not had the impact that we'd hope? To answer these questions, we need to acknowledge that there are several problems with research in education. These are not reasons to turn a blind eye to research, or to dismiss it. They are simply a set of warning lights for you to be aware of when reading, interpreting and implementing research in your classroom.

## ACCESSIBILITY

Until recently, many research studies were hidden away from the busy classroom teacher in research papers. Although they weren't under lock and key, you had to know what you were looking for and how to get your hands on it. Many teachers simply did not know that these studies existed and didn't have the time to spend hours trawling university libraries for potential studies relating to learning. In recent years this situation has improved enormously thanks to digital technology and the accessibility of almost anything you want to find on the internet. This has been further helped by the growing number of charities and organisations specialising in educational research with the simple goal of making it more accessible to teachers and schools. Nevertheless, it can sometimes still be tricky to get hold of certain research papers, which may sit behind a paywall, and some teachers still may not be aware of the avenues available to them to access research.

## LENGTH AND LANGUAGE

Due to the very nature of our busy roles as teachers and school leaders, having to wade through a 500-page research paper written in the language of academia may not be that appealing or accessible. Our challenge is to give our teachers access to key studies and theories in bite-sized chunks. Teachers don't need to do the research (it's been done for us and in far more reliable conditions than we could ever construct); they just need to have knowledge of it and use it to increase the effectiveness of their classroom practice. It is the job of school leaders and the educational research organisations mentioned on page xi to filter all the research that's now available to us. They must condense it into easy-to-understand chunks, before helping to develop teachers' understanding of it, so they can adapt their practices accordingly.

## CONFIRMATION BIAS

One of the other reasons that teachers may have struggled to engage with research can be explained through confirmation bias theory. This is a cognitive bias that typically involves favouring or searching for information that confirms your existing beliefs. How this plays out in the classroom is that we tend to notice the positive impact of things we believe in already. For example, if you have a deep-seated belief that getting students to work in groups is the best way to structure learning tasks, you'll take heart from every positive that this demonstrates, choosing subconsciously to forget the moments when it negatively interferes with learning. The same also applies when searching for research, or indeed choosing not to search for it. We are far more likely to search for evidence that backs up our beliefs than consciously look for evidence to discredit our beliefs. Therefore, when you believe that a teaching strategy is the best way forward (even if your belief has just been formulated by folklore), you are unlikely to want to challenge your beliefs based on a research study written by a university professor 50 years ago. And, even if you happen to stumble across some research that contradicts your beliefs and assumptions, it can be easy to dismiss because 'it obviously wasn't conducted on the type of students I teach'.

## MISCONCEPTIONS OF RESEARCH

One of the major problems with educational research in recent years is that misconceptions can be caused by individuals interpreting the research in different ways and third parties intentionally or unintentionally miscommunicating the findings. In some cases, this is because we try to infer things from the research that were not originally intended (this can be due to confirmation bias), or because we haven't fully understood the purpose or intentions of the study. Quite often this can come from only reading the headline results and making our own minds up about what the study involved or why the results ended up like they did. In other cases, it can be because media outlets or influential voices take parts of the research findings and twist their meaning, intentionally misleading people to help back up a certain message.

The most commonly cited example of this in education is how schools interpreted the original research from the Sutton Trust in 2011 relating to the fact that feedback is one of the most important and significant interventions that a teacher can use to improve student learning. Schools across the country took this as meaning more marking. But, if you look at the research, it continuously uses the term 'feedback' and not the word 'marking'. What happened was a significant increase on the demands of teachers away from school, marking books and writing copious amounts of comments on every piece of work, only to find out nearly a decade later that the vast amount of written comments that teachers make in student books have 'almost no effect on student achievement' (Wiliam in Hendrick and Macpherson, 2017).

## WHAT 'WORKED', NOT NECESSARILY WHAT 'WORKS'

By the very nature of what research is, it reports on what has worked previously, with a strong evidence base to demonstrate its reliability. However, what it doesn't do is accurately predict what will work in the future. Just because something has worked somewhere, it doesn't mean that it will work somewhere else, or even again in the same setting. To help combat this, the term 'best bets' is starting to appear in the language of educational research to help us recognise that results might not always be reproduced perfectly and recommendations are certainly not a guaranteed success; instead the research presents your 'best bet' of helping students learn in your classroom. In the UK, teachers are exposed to these 'best bets' by the *Sutton Trust-EEF Teaching and Learning Toolkit* (Education Endowment Foundation, 2012; https://educationendowmentfoundation.org.uk/evidence-summaries/teaching-learning-toolkit) and in the US, this is supported by the What Works Clearinghouse website (https://ies.ed.gov/ncee/wwc).

## CONTEXT

Finally, the biggest problem that teachers have when trying to apply educational research to their own classroom setting is context. Every school is different and, in some cases, classes can be very different from one another within the same school. This means that it is very difficult to simply pick a piece of research off the shelf, plug it in to your own context and expect it to have the same impact as it did when it was originally trialled and tested. That is not to say that it might not have the same impact, but you need to look very carefully at the specific conditions in which it was set up. Are your conditions the same? And what might have been helping it to work, compared to what might be preventing it from working so well in your own setting? This external validity is crucial when thinking about dropping a piece of research or a strategy that has been borne from that research into your school. In simple terms, how well will this research travel?

Despite these problems, it is essential that we, as a profession, make a concerted effort to engage in the research behind how humans learn. It can be easy to dismiss something because you were too busy to read it or it wasn't trialled with your students, but if we persist in burying our heads in the sand when it comes to the science of learning, we will continue to waste time, energy and money whilst squandering the life chances of the young people in our care.

Now is the time to reboot teaching with the science of learning. Let's reboot our profession together.

# HOW TO USE THIS BOOK

*Teaching Rebooted* aims to provide you with an accessible and concise overview of the main research that underpins how we learn as human beings. The chapters are intended to challenge your thinking, helping you reflect on what you may have been doing in your classroom and the impact of this on student progress and achievement. Across ten chapters, the book provides 40 ideas and strategies to help you turn the 'evidence-based research' presented into 'research-informed practice' the very next day.

Every chapter considers a specific teaching strategy that we know has a firm evidence base and will help guide classroom practice. Although you may wish to read the book from front to back, it is designed to enable you to dip in and out of the various chapters when you need to, depending on the area of research that you may be interested in at any given point in time.

Each chapter in *Teaching Rebooted* follows the same format for ease of use and includes the following sections.

## TEACHER 1.0

A frank examination of how we've been misguided in our classroom approach by using common teaching strategies and school policies that may not be in tune with what evidence-based research tells us about how students learn most efficiently and effectively. This section considers some of the bad habits that have developed in our schools, stemming from a lack of awareness about the science of learning.

## WHAT DOES THE RESEARCH SAY?

A succinct overview of the main research that underpins the teaching strategy in question and the implications this has for teachers, school leaders, students and parents. Throughout this section, the essential information from the research is highlighted in boxes, so look out for the key symbol if you're really short on time.

# TEACHER 2.0

**2.0**

A selection of practical and easy-to-implement ideas that you can use with your students the very next day. These are research-informed strategies that will help you to implement the evidence-based principles outlined in the chapter. There is a total of **40 practical strategies** to pick up and use throughout the book. Each idea ends with a teaching tip to help you put the idea into practice.

Just be aware that implementation is the key to success. Even poor strategies can work to some extent if you put enough time and effort into them. Similarly, if you implement a great strategy poorly, it won't have the impact you were hoping for.

# FURTHER READING

Although the main research is broken down into an easy-to-digest summary in 'What does the research say?', each chapter also provides suggestions for further reading. This includes researchers whose work you might want to explore further, reports you may want to read in full and keywords you can put into a search engine if you want to take a deeper dive into the research.

# PERSONAL REFLECTION

At the end of each chapter, there are several reflective questions to challenge your thinking. These relate to what you may have done previously in your classroom and how the evidence-based research may influence your classroom practice in the future.

# CHAPTER 1

# RETRIEVAL PRACTICE

Retrieval practice is the act of recalling information from memory in order to make the memory of that information even stronger. In this chapter we will focus on the research behind retrieval practice, together with how you can implement and integrate this strategy into your classroom practice to improve students' retention of knowledge.

# TEACHER 1.0

**1.0**

Teachers have always tested students on what they do or do not know, for as long as schools have existed. This certainly isn't a new phenomenon in education. Think back to your own days at school and you'll quickly be reminded of teachers testing you on the knowledge you had supposedly acquired over the preceding lessons. In most cases, testing students to remember what they had been taught was simply a vehicle to identify where the gaps in their knowledge were, whilst also providing sufficient data to be able to rank students by grade, level or percentage. In more recent times, when accountability measures have been significantly heightened and the whole educational community has become obsessed with tracking numerical progress data, testing has enabled teachers to generate regular scores to enter into numerous spreadsheets that are colour coded, RAG rated and analysed to the nth degree.

In the best cases of using testing to generate student performance data, this has been the catalyst for responsive teaching, where gaps in knowledge are identified and then lessons are adapted accordingly. However, in the worst cases it has just been the medium to enable a teacher to fulfil a data capture that has been imposed on them by a senior leadership team. Think about the number of times nothing happens after the data has been inputted into a spreadsheet. Hours and hours have been spent marking assessments and then painstakingly adding all of the scores to an electronic tracker or spreadsheet, but crucially nothing different happens in the classroom as a result of the assessment. There isn't a single student on the planet who has improved simply because their test score has been written down somewhere.

One thing that most people would tell you is that getting students to revise before a test made testing a useful learning tool. This was generally seen as the major positive in getting students to recall prior knowledge – they had to revise this knowledge in the first place. All too often though, this led to students cramming their 'revision' into a couple of hours the night before a pre-determined test date. They could fairly successfully reproduce information from their short-term memory but it would be forgotten just hours after the test. As we will discover from the research, most teachers were missing the fact that the most important feature in the whole process of testing is the actual act of trying to retrieve the information, not the final 'performance' of a student recorded in a mark book or spreadsheet.

# WHAT DOES THE RESEARCH SAY?

Although there have been multiple studies conducted in this area, I am going to focus on two sources of research that I believe are the most powerful for teachers and senior leaders at all levels to be able to digest and put into practice:

▶ Robert A. Bjork (1975), 'Retrieval as a memory modifier: An interpretation of negative recency and related phenomena', in Robert L. Solso (ed.), *Information Processing and Cognition: The Loyola Symposium*, pp. 123–144. New York, NY: Lawrence Erlbaum.

▶ Henry L. Roediger and Jeffrey D. Karpicke (2006), 'Test-enhanced learning: Taking memory tests improves long-term retention', *Psychological Science*, 17, (3), 249–255.

## ROBERT AND ELIZABETH BJORK

Although Robert Bjork's 1975 paper is cited as one of the first key papers he wrote on memory and retrieval practice, Robert and Elizabeth Bjork's subsequent papers, interviews and work to date all centre around the same core ideas that have since been rigorously tested, developed and written about even further. Their work on human memory is commonly cited as being some of the most universally accepted and pivotal studies for us to learn from when it comes to how the human brain retains information. Even though these studies began 45 years ago, they are just as important and accurate today as they were then.

Throughout their work over the past few decades, Bjork and Bjork's key message is that taking a test often does more than assess knowledge, and that, in most cases, testing can provide opportunities for learning. The reason behind this is that when information is successfully retrieved from our memory, it becomes more recallable in the future. The more often we retrieve this information, the easier it becomes to retrieve it. Each retrieval makes the information more easily accessible in our memory. Therefore, the more opportunities we can give our students to practise actively recalling information, the stronger their memory of it will become. What this means in the classroom is that getting students to produce something from memory, rather than just presenting them with information, greatly increases the chance of it being consigned to the student's long-term memory. In short, the act of actually retrieving information from our memory is the key part of the learning process, not the final performance in a test.

**The more often we recall information, the easier it is to recall it in the future.**

Interestingly, Bjork and Bjork also stress that the more difficult the retrieval, the stronger the memory trace, demonstrating how, with the right conditions and 'desirable difficulties' built in, skilfully implemented retrieval practice promotes long-term retention. What this means in practice is that students need a chance to forget information before they try to retrieve it. Asking students to recall what they did at the start of the lesson or even what they did yesterday or last week is relatively easy. Student performance will generally show high success rates of retrieval in these situations, but this will reduce dramatically as time goes on, with students remembering little or nothing if you tested them on the same information in four or five weeks' time. Bjork and Bjork make the point that by introducing time to forget this content before it is tested or reintroduced, the initial short-term performance might drop but the long-term learning will be significantly increased due to the act of having to retrieve information under more difficult conditions.

 **The more difficult the retrieval is, the stronger the memory trace becomes. Students need a chance to forget information before they retrieve it.**

Although this sounds eminently sensible, Bjork and Bjork do warn us of the fact that students won't particularly like this change in testing and recall. If previously they have been asked to recall information from their short-term memory and have had relatively high success rates in doing so, asking them now to recall information they may have forgotten will undoubtedly produce lower performance scores to begin with and have a knock-on effect on their confidence and levels of enjoyment. It is therefore imperative to explain to students the fundamental reasons behind effective retrieval practice and how the 'desirable difficulties' you are imposing on them are for the benefit of long-term learning, not just short-term performance.

When speaking to students about how to manage their studies effectively, Robert Bjork often says he uses the phrase 'input less and output more'. Bjork says that if students could get into the regular habit of practising producing information from memory by answering questions, they would be far more successful in assessment environments when examinations cover content that has been taught or presented to students over a significant period of time. If students also understand the importance of applying their own set of desirable difficulties to their learning, and get parents or friends to quiz them on content that they haven't just learned, their ability to transfer knowledge to their long-term memory and then recall it at a later date will be greatly enhanced.

# HENRY L. ROEDIGER III AND JEFFREY D. KARPICKE

Roediger and Karpicke build on the research from Robert and Elizabeth Bjork and many others on 'retrieval practice' and what they refer to as the 'testing effect' – the fact that our long-term memory of a specific set of information is strengthened by regular retrieval or testing. Roediger and Karpicke have noted some interesting findings on the relationship between testing and restudying material in the classroom and the impact they both have on long-term learning. Their 2006 research article 'Test-enhanced learning: Taking memory tests improves long-term retention' is often cited as a key research study in the field of memory.

In their research trial and laboratory testing, Roediger and Karpicke found that additional studying can produce better retention in the short term and increase students' confidence in their ability to remember material. However, on delayed tests (where students were tested on prior learning after a period of forgetting), re-studying is significantly surpassed by regular retrieval practice and testing, producing far better long-term retention of that material. Their results show that testing (and not studying) is the critical factor for promoting long-term recall. Not only that, but their research trial also demonstrated that repeated study after one successful recall did not produce any measurable learning a week later. In short, they found that repeated studying once an item has been recalled produces essentially no benefit. This may be, in part, due to a false sense of fluency that students have when they re-study something that they have already seen before, mistaking familiarity with deep learning. Re-studying, or revision, feels easy because students are only surface reading their own notes, believing they already know it because their brain recognises the material. This adds even more weight and value to Bjork and Bjork's conclusion that testing subject content is in fact a powerful means of improving learning, not just a neutral process for assessing the contents of a student's memory as many teachers believe.

 **Testing is a powerful way to improve learning, not just a vehicle for assessing it.**

Roediger and Karpicke also questioned many students as part of their research to gain an understanding of the strategies they preferred to use to study for exams. The overwhelming response was that practising recall through a process of self-testing was a seldom-used strategy. Even when students reported that they did test themselves during periods of study, their motivation was to assess purely what they had or had not learned, rather than to enhance their long-term memory. More worryingly, the general consensus that Roediger and Karpicke found between students and teachers on retrieval practice was that if information can be recalled successfully from memory once, it must have been learned and can therefore be dropped from further retrieval practice in order to prioritise other content. However, all of the research around retrieval practice and long-term memory clearly demonstrates that, even after items can be recalled from memory, regular testing and recall opportunities must still take place in order to transfer that information from the short-term memory into the long-term memory. Without this, the memory of that material will significantly fade over time.

 **Testing, and not re-studying, is the best way to enhance long-term memory.**

# TEACHER 2.0

Now we understand that retrieval practice is one of the most powerful tools in the learning process, it's clear that it should form an essential part of your lessons. Let's take a look at some easy-to-implement strategies that you can use to embed retrieval practice and reboot your teaching – starting tomorrow!

 ## IDEA 1: LOW-STAKES LESSON SUMMARY QUIZ

### *Find out if they can tell you what you've just taught them.*

If you are just dipping your toe in the water with retrieval practice, start with a simple but effective lesson summary quiz. If you think that just because you've taught it the students will remember it, you may need to think again. You'll be amazed at how much students will have forgotten even by the end of a lesson. Linking back to the research from both Bjork and Bjork, and Roediger and Karpicke, if you don't ask your students to practise recalling this information, it will slowly slip out of their short-term memory and they will be unable to recall it in the future.

A simple five- or ten-question low-stakes quiz at the end of the lesson, based on the material you have just taught, is a great way to activate students' brains into recalling that information, giving it a far higher chance of sticking when you see them next. However, the trick is in the title; it has to be low stakes. This is not about who gets the best score and you should not be recording scores in your mark book or in a spreadsheet. Remember – the learning is in the process, not in recording the grades. Students need to value the activity as a learning tool, not as an assessment of performance. Getting things wrong is not a problem in the first instance. The fact that they have had to think about the subject material, and try to retrieve it, is all part of them being able to memorise it more effectively in the future.

If your regular quizzes become too competitive and high stakes, students will be fearful of them and become anxious or nervous about testing. If this happens, students can begin to freeze in testing situations. Even worse, they may decide that not trying at all is better than trying and getting something wrong, because they are concerned about being perceived as 'stupid' or about the consequences of not performing in line with expectations. Your job is to make students understand the benefit of your low-stakes quizzing, so that they are not only comfortable taking part and using their brain to activate their prior learning, but also more likely to take part in this type of activity independently at home when studying or revising for their exams.

> **TEACHING TIP**
>
> *The questions don't always have to come from you. Why not ask the students to create their own questions from time to time, so that they can ask their partner a few questions on what they have just learned? This way you get the added benefit of the students first reviewing the lesson content in order to create some questions, before they have to answer questions from their partner.*

## IDEA 2: LOW-STAKES REVIEW OF LAST LESSON

### *Can you remember what we did yesterday?*

Now try to add some desirable difficulties into your low-stakes quizzing by setting a series of questions on the previous lesson that you taught. This way you are beginning to allow students some time to forget the material before you ask them to recall it. Your level of desirable difficulty will be higher or lower depending on the number of times you see your class every week. For example, an English or maths teacher who might see their class several times per week might feel that this information is still relatively easy to retrieve, because there may be only 24 hours between teaching and testing. However, in some other subjects, where students only have that lesson once or twice per fortnight, the time between teaching and testing can be greatly increased, creating significant time to forget the material, thus increasing the desirable difficulty of the quiz.

The easiest way to implement these review quizzes is as part of your starter activity. By having a set of pre-prepared questions relating to your last lesson, you can easily either distribute them at the start of your lesson or have them on the board as a bell activity for students to complete the second they enter your classroom. Not only does this help to settle the class and give you time to complete your 'housekeeping' tasks like taking the register, it also helps to focus your students' minds on their learning, whilst providing an extremely efficient way of helping to make what you taught last lesson stick. This is even more useful if your lesson today builds on the lesson from yesterday and your students need to use their prior learning to help them understand key concepts.

Just as the previous idea, this needs to be a low-stakes quiz where no marks are recorded. It is fine to go through the correct answers with students at the end of the quiz, but the emphasis should be on the learning gains, not individual student performance. However, even though this is low stakes, students should still be working in silence, providing each and every one of them with an environment in which to think hard, without the distractions of other people talking. Only under these conditions can we effectively engage our brain in activating prior learning from memory.

**TEACHING TIP**

*If you only taught your class the previous day, the way to make your quiz a little more difficult is to set it at the end of the lesson and not the start. This way, the information that they are retrieving is not right at the front of their short-term memory. The content that you will have taught them today will have started to push yesterday's information further back in their mind, thus making the quiz more desirably difficult.*

# IDEA 3: LAST LESSON, LAST MONTH, LAST UNIT

## *How much can you remember from this unit of work?*

If you want to increase the level of desirable difficulty even further, try setting a quiz that is not exclusive to the learning from one lesson. Set ten questions that cover some subject material from last lesson, together with a selection of material you taught them last month, and culminating with one or two questions from a previous topic. This way, you begin to really work on students being tested on material that they have had time to forget. This can quite easily become your start- or end-of-lesson routine, where students work quietly for a set amount of time on the questions you either read out to them or provide them with on the board or on paper. If you hand the questions out on paper, ask students to keep them in their books. These questions can then be used at a later stage by the students themselves for self-quizzing or by their parents or friends to test them.

You might want to split the quiz into sections so that students can clearly see which questions are from last lesson, last month and the last unit, demonstrating that the longer ago something was taught, the harder it is to recall. This can help you explain the rationale behind quizzing them on previous material and imposing these levels of desirable difficulty on them. When students compare their scores on each section, it might start to emphasise the need to do more self-quizzing on material that has been taught and now forgotten, rather than just material that is in the short-term memory and therefore easily retrievable.

As with the previous two ideas, there is no need to record any scores. The learning is in the act of trying to retrieve previously taught information.

> **TEACHING TIP**
> *If you want to combine a few different retrieval strategies, why not use this quizzing strategy once a fortnight, so that you can still use the previous two strategies as well? Students will then know to expect this quiz to be more difficult, due to the information that you are going to be asking them to recall. This also allows you to keep your recall activities fresh so that the students don't get bored of the same type of quiz every lesson.*

# IDEA 4: BRAIN DUMP

*Tell me everything you know on this topic.*

Taking retrieval practice one step further, a 'brain dump' is a great way to get students to activate their prior learning and recall everything they know on a topic. In this scenario, a student starts with a blank piece of paper and simply writes down everything they know and can remember on a certain topic. Students are free to record their information in any way they choose – spider diagram, bullet points, mind map, written prose, and so on.

The beauty of this retrieval task is twofold. Firstly, students can use whichever style they want to record their prior knowledge. They are not penalised by a certain way of expressing their knowledge. The learning is in the fact that they are literally dumping everything that's in their brain about a certain topic onto a blank page. We all have our favoured ways of doing this, so we shouldn't prescribe a specific method to our students. As long as they are retrieving this information from their long-term memory, the task will have a significant impact on their ability to recall it again at a later date. Secondly, because they are not answering a specific question, students can retrieve far more information than any one question could ask for, meaning that, if used well, this activity can be an extremely useful learning tool. We've all seen before when a student knows the information but gets tripped up by the way a question is written. This way, there is no question to trip anybody up, or limit what they can recall and write about.

Brain dumps can be introduced at any point in the lesson to promote the recall of prior knowledge. They can be used at the start, middle or end of a lesson and can focus on any topic that students have previously studied and have had time to forget. The more time that has passed since they have studied the topic, the greater the desirable difficulty.

**TEACHING TIP**

*To add a further level of desirable difficulty to this strategy, why not set a timer of three or four minutes for students to complete their brain dumps? This forces students to focus carefully on the task in hand and it gets them to prioritise the information and not how they are going to present it. It's far better to have more information being recalled and written on the paper, even if it's just in bullet points, rather than a wonderfully colourful and creative mind map with only a couple of bits of information on it.*

# FURTHER READING

If you want to take a deeper dive into the research around retrieval practice, here are some useful starting points.

▶ **Researchers:** Robert A. Bjork, Elizabeth L. Bjork, Henry L. Roediger III, Jeffrey D. Karpicke, Robert Coe, Megan Sumeraki, Yana Weinstein.

▶ **Publications:** Robert A. Bjork (1975), 'Retrieval as a memory modifier: An interpretation of negative recency and related phenomena', in Robert L. Solso (ed.), *Information Processing and Cognition: The Loyola Symposium*, pp. 123–44. New York, NY: Lawrence Erlbaum.

Henry L. Roediger and Jeffrey D. Karpicke (2006), 'Test-enhanced learning: Taking memory tests improves long-term retention', *Psychological Science*, 17, (3), 249–255.

Robert Coe (2020), 'Does research on retrieval practice translate into classroom practice?', *Impact*, (8).

Megan Sumeraki and Yana Weinstein (2018), 'Optimising learning using retrieval practice', *Impact*, (2).

▶ **Keyword search:** Retrieval practice; testing effect; memory; recall; desirable difficulties.

# PERSONAL REFLECTION

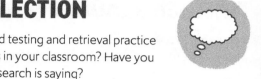

How have you previously used testing and retrieval practice as part of the learning process in your classroom? Have you been in tune with what the research is saying?

How might you now utilise the power of retrieval practice in your classroom?

# CHAPTER 2

# SPACING

Spacing is the length of time that you leave between the first time you teach information and then asking students to recall that information or do something with it. In this chapter we will take a look at the research behind effective and intelligent spacing and how it can have a significant impact on long-term learning and not just short-term performance.

# TEACHER 1.0

**1.0**

Structuring how we sequence our lessons and teach the curriculum content that we have to get through has previously been a relatively simple process. Most of us would probably recognise (either from how we have been taught ourselves as students at school, or how we began to teach as qualified teachers) a model of teaching a specific unit of work from start to finish and then assessing student understanding at the end of it. In broad and simplistic terms, this has always seemed perfectly sensible: devote your sole focus to teaching a set topic and then assess students on what they have learned before you move on to the next topic. I can vividly remember thinking to myself when I first started teaching that, if I left an assessment too long, the students would have forgotten what I had taught them, resulting in poorer performance on the assessment.

It has only been through the research that we will discuss on page 15 that we have now started to discover that actually giving students time to forget things might actually enhance learning and not detract from it. By 'blocking' all of our lesson content in sequential lessons and then assessing understanding immediately afterwards, students have not been provided with sufficient 'desirable difficulty' (see page 8). This means that their 'performance' on the final assessment has been significantly influenced not by what they have actually learned but by what has been sitting in their short-term memory. The assumptions we have been making about how much students have actually 'learned' have been wildly inaccurate for far too long. As we will discuss in Chapter 7 on 'Learning versus performance' (page 77), many teachers in schools have been assessing performance as opposed to real learning.

The blocking of subject content, followed by an immediate assessment, has also caused some significant inaccuracies in predicting student outcomes at the end of a course. Take, for example, the typical student who has 'performed' quite well on their end-of-unit tests throughout the course, but has not had the opportunity to revisit certain concepts and be tested on what he or she did six months ago, not just six weeks ago. Far too many times we have seen that student, at the eleventh hour, suddenly move from being on track at every checkpoint to significantly underachieving at the final hurdle. This lack of consideration for giving students time to forget something and instead 'blocking' or 'massing' content together has been a fixture of many school curricula for decades and has not done anything to help embed deep and sustainable learning.

# WHAT DOES THE RESEARCH SAY?

Spacing and retrieval practice are intrinsically linked. Research in these areas is often combined and published together as part of one study; you can't really discuss best practice in retrieval practice without any mention of spacing. We'll therefore be returning to the work of Robert and Elizabeth Bjork, whom we met in Chapter 1, but we'll begin by exploring one of the most influential pieces of cognitive science research of all time, a study that was already over 100 years old when I started secondary school as a student in 1988:

▶ Hermann Ebbinghaus (1885), 'The forgetting curve' in *Memory: A contribution to experimental psychology*. New York, NY: Teachers College, Columbia University.

▶ Elizabeth L. Bjork and Robert A. Bjork (2011), Bjork, E. L. and Bjork, R. A. (2014), 'Making things hard on yourself, but in a good way: Creating desirable difficulties to enhance learning', in M. A. Gernsbacher and J. Pomerantz (eds.), *Psychology and the Real World: Essays illustrating fundamental contributions to society* (2nd edn.), (pp. 59-68). New York, NY: Worth.

## HERMANN EBBINGHAUS (EBBINGHAUS'S 'FORGETTING CURVE')

Way back in 1885, Hermann Ebbinghaus conducted a pioneering piece of research on the human mind, investigating how successfully we are able to retain information. Little did he know at the time that his findings would prove to be one of the most talked about and referenced research studies on the human mind of all time. In his experiment, Ebbinghaus conducted a series of tests on himself, memorising a number of meaningless three-letter words over a period of time. Ebbinghaus then tested himself to see if he could recall and retain the information after a varying degree of different time periods. The results he obtained were plotted in the graph on the following page, which is now referred to as the 'Forgetting Curve'.

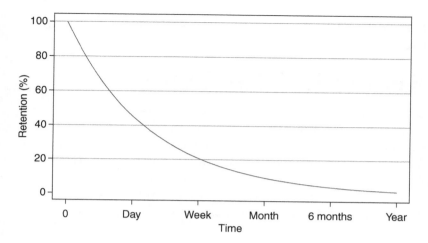

Ebbinghaus found the Forgetting Curve to be exponential in nature. His results demonstrated that memory retention is 100 per cent at the time of learning, but that it drops rapidly by around 40 per cent within the first few days and nearly 90 per cent within the first month. After this point, memory retention continues to decline, but decreases at a much slower rate.

 **You forget 40 per cent of the information you have been taught within the first day, and 90 per cent within a month.**

Linking to retrieval practice and the 'testing effect' that we examined in Chapter 1, page 5, Ebbinghaus discovered that, although our ability to recall information decreases rapidly after the initial input, the more we reinforce the initial input with spaced retrieval practice, the stronger our memory of that information becomes. This begins to reduce the rate at which we lose that initial information. To put it bluntly – you use it or you lose it.

 **You must use information or you will lose it.**

Ebbinghaus thus began to deduce a theory (which many more recent cognitive scientists have now developed even further) that the only way to combat this decline in memory retention is to revisit and actively recall the material at various intervals after the initial input. His work led him to believe that each act of recalling such information enables us to increase the interval for when the next act of recall is required. Once we begin to increase the length of time between the input and our retrieval (as long as we are successful in this retrieval), the stronger our memory becomes. This began to be the foundation for many future studies on testing, retrieval practice and human memory.

**The longer we leave between each successful recall of information, the stronger our memory of that information becomes.**

## ROBERT AND ELIZABETH BJORK

In Chapter 1, page 4, we referred to the need to impose 'desirable difficulties' upon our students in order to create the best and most fertile conditions for learning to be sustained over time. This is one of the fundamental areas that underpin Bjork and Bjork's work on memory, and the idea of 'spacing' (influenced by Hermann Ebbinghaus over 125 years earlier) is one of their key components within this. In their paper 'Making things hard on yourself, but in a good way: Creating desirable difficulties to enhance learning', Robert and Elizabeth Bjork (2014) are quick to emphasise that there is a skill in ensuring that your difficulties are desirable and not undesirable. Without a student having sufficient background knowledge in order to respond to the difficulties that you impose, the difficulties will quickly become undesirable and result in a lack of motivation. Just like how you pitch a lesson: if it is too easy there is no learning, and if it is way too hard students can switch off. Getting the right amount of spacing between the input and future retrieval attempts is absolutely key.

**Spacing is a great way to impose a desirable difficulty upon your learners, which will result in stronger long-term memory retention.**

Bjork and Bjork (2011) point out that there have been a myriad of studies conducted on the spacing effect, and consequently it is 'one of the most general and robust effects from across the entire history of experimental research on learning and memory'. This immediately demonstrates how important it is for all teachers to understand this theory, but it also calls into question why our traditional method of 'blocking' or 'massing' content has been accepted as good practice for so long. Bjork and Bjork go some way to explaining why this might be. They conclude that not only is 'blocking' or 'massing' repeated study activities convenient for teachers and curriculum designers, but it also frequently results in rapid gains in apparent learning. We can all relate to the fact that an all-night cramming session can go some way to producing a good test 'performance' the next morning. However, little of what was recallable on the day of the test will remain recallable over time. In contrast, a study schedule that spaces or distributes study sessions, allowing time for content to be forgotten before it is recalled, can produce both good exam performance and good long-term retention.

 **'Blocking' or 'massing' might initially produce rapid gains in apparent learning, but spaced practice produces far better long-term learning.**

The immediate 'performance' gains that can be attributed to blocked practice or late-night cramming before a test are the nemesis to spacing. Students will tell you that they prefer blocked practice for two reasons:

1.  As mentioned in Chapter 1, page 4, students feel far more confident practising the same content in a massed scenario. As Bjork and Bjork have uncovered, prior exposure to something creates a sense of familiarity that can easily be confused with understanding. However, just because they recognise content doesn't mean to say that they will be able to recall it at a later date.

2.  The traditional method of blocked or massed practice does produce better short-term performance gains. Bjork and Bjork are very clear that all previous studies on spacing (which can also be referred to as distributed practice) versus blocked or massed practice have demonstrated this. However, as we now know, this is to the detriment of long-term learning and sustainable knowledge. Students will want to opt for this traditional method of learning when they can see immediate short-term improvements in assessment results. During study periods, a student's confidence is directly linked to how they are performing and the immediate output that they see from the hours that they have put in. In this way, they will always favour short-term performance indicators, rather than trusting a longer-term process.

It is therefore crucial to take the time to explain the highlights of this research to your students, so that they don't keep falling into the same traps of improving short-term 'performance', but not strengthening their long-term learning.

# TEACHER 2.0

These research studies should form the foundation of our strategic decisions as teachers, so let's take a look at some ways you can use spacing in your classroom.

### IDEA 5: CUMULATIVE TESTING

*We're going to have regular tests on everything that I've taught you so far.*

The easiest way to implement spacing in your regular classroom practice is to combine both spacing and retrieval practice and ensure that any end-of-unit tests or assessments are cumulative. If your tests only assess understanding of one topic at a time, it becomes extremely difficult for students to retrieve information successfully from previous units. Without cumulative testing, you are only assessing the performance of a student on one specific unit and not how much they have learned and remembered throughout the duration of the course.

The process is simple. Every time you plan an assessment or test on a particular unit, include some content from the previous unit. This should then continue as the course progresses. For example, at the end of Unit 2, you should include questions from Units 1 and 2. Then, at the end of Unit 3, you should include questions from Units 1, 2 and 3. Depending on the ability of the class and the level of desirable difficulty required, you can decide how many questions to include from previous units. The more you include from more distant units, the more difficult it will be. If students are able to recall this information, then the stronger their memory of it will become and the more easily they will be able to recall it in the future.

If you are using some of the low-stakes quizzing techniques from Chapter 1 already, you may decide to record the results as part of your formal testing. By testing students on everything that you have taught at regular intervals, the accuracy of your recorded assessments should be far greater.

**TEACHING TIP**

*Select the most important information that students need to know from previous units for your cumulative testing. By mapping out what you want to get students to recall from previous units, you can ensure that the key content is revisited and recalled sufficiently throughout the course of the year.*

# IDEA 6: LAGGED HOMEWORK

### *Can you apply the information that I gave you in the previous unit to this task tonight?*

If you want to add even more space between your input and recall, you may want to think about setting lagged homework tasks. Traditionally teachers would set a homework task based on the topic they are teaching or a lesson that they have just taught that day. However, that does not follow any of the underlying principles of research that we now know about. Without giving students any time to forget the information, the homework becomes relatively easy because the knowledge they require to perform or complete the task is still stored in their short-term memory.

With lagged homework, you plan to set a task, which is related to the topic you have taught, at some point in the future. To begin with, this may be only a week in the future, when Ebbinghaus's Forgetting Curve suggests that students may have forgotten almost 80 per cent of what you have taught. However, once your students are used to this new practice, and you have taken the time to speak to them about why you are doing it and the benefits it will have on their retention of this information in the future, you may begin to schedule even longer gaps. In practice, this might involve teaching a topic in Week 3, but setting a lagged homework task on that topic three or four weeks later in Week 7.

If you want to increase the level of desirable difficulty even further, simply allow more time between teaching the topic and setting the lagged homework task, or you may want to revisit the topic for a second homework task in a few months' time.

**TEACHING TIP**

*If you start setting lagged homework without explaining to the students why you are doing this and the benefit it has on their learning and long-term memory, they will get pretty frustrated. By talking to them about the science behind your strategy, you can head off a multitude of questions from the students (and even some of their parents) about why you are setting a task related to something they may have already forgotten about.*

# IDEA 7: SEQUENCING OF LESSONS

## Why this and why now?

Thinking about how you sequence your lessons using spacing, rather than just 'blocking' them all together in one unit, can be quite a tricky thing to do as a teacher, but can reap significant rewards in terms of long-term learning. This isn't as straight forward as simply adding some spacing in between your input and your recall activities, as in the previous two ideas. It involves far more thought and consideration about how you plan out what you are going to deliver and when. As we know from the research by Robert and Elizabeth Bjork, spacing out some of the content that you teach, and giving students time to forget some of it, adds a level of desirable difficulty to your delivery, because it makes your students' brains work much harder than they would if they were already familiar with it.

Sitting down with your medium- and long-term plan, together with your scheme of learning, you will be able to intelligently schedule your sequencing of lessons using the principles that we have discussed in the research section of this chapter on page 15.

However, one thing that all of the cognitive scientists seem to agree on when looking at how to put this into practice is that a blocked structure of delivery is probably best when teaching novice learners (whether they are new to a topic or have limited experience or knowledge on which to draw). In this scenario, spacing out your delivery is too much of a desirable difficulty and starts to move into the territory of an undesirable difficulty. But, once they establish some of the fundamental knowledge required to be successful in your subject, a spaced approach to learning will have far more benefits in long-term learning and knowledge retention.

> **TEACHING TIP**
>
> *Don't be afraid to change the sequence of your lessons once you establish the ability and background knowledge of your students. If you feel that they are still novice learners and need the safe repetition of the same content back to back, then keep it like that. However, if you feel that they have the foundation knowledge and maturity to take on a more difficult and intelligently structured approach to learning, why not reshuffle your pack?*

# IDEA 8: STUDENT STUDY SCHEDULES

## Get students to take ownership of their independent study.

Outside of the classroom, students themselves can use the principle of spacing to become more effective independent learners. By introducing a regular spaced study schedule, students can implement the theory of spacing in their own homes, meaning that regular opportunities for revisiting class content and retrieving this information can be systematically built in throughout the academic year. For most students, you may have to model this for them in school to begin with and even provide them with blank or partly populated study schedules for them to use. By providing a template study schedule, you can walk and talk your students through exactly how to use it, getting them to begin to complete it under your watchful eye. Students can then take them home, pin them up in their bedroom and begin to use them.

Make sure you share with your students why spacing is important and the basic theories behind spacing and retrieval practice; otherwise the study schedule will quickly become something that they just forget and don't use. The trick is to talk them through (either as a class teacher for your own group, or as a senior leader for a whole year group) the benefits that these methods have in terms of their ability to retain information. Most students will be all ears if you can tell them how to work smarter and not harder. You may also want to briefly introduce them to Ebbinghaus's Forgetting Curve, so that they can create their own spacing schedules based on when they will start to forget the initial information that they have been given in class. With Ebbinghaus's research being shown in a simple-to-understand graph, the concept will be far easier for students to grasp due to its visual nature.

Going one step further with study schedules, you may also want to monitor them from time to time to ensure that they are still being used, way past any study schedule honeymoon period that may exist. An easy way to do this is for students to bring them in and talk you through them, explaining to you when they are doing independent study and why they have chosen to schedule or space out their study as they have. Getting students to verbalise this to you helps them understand the reasons behind their strategic scheduling and reiterates that it is all part of a scientific process, not just a game of random scheduling.

# FURTHER READING

If you want to continue your reading into the research around spacing and its practical uses in the classroom, here are some useful starting points.

▶ **Researchers:** Hermann Ebbinghaus, Robert A. Bjork, Elizabeth L. Bjork, Jonathan Firth, Christopher N. Wahlheim, John Dunlosky, Larry L. Jacoby.

▶ **Publications:** Hermann Ebbinghaus (1885), 'The forgetting curve' in *Memory: A contribution to experimental psychology*. New York, NY: Teachers College, Columbia University.

Elizabeth L. Bjork and Robert A. Bjork (2014), 'Making things hard on yourself, but in a good way: Creating desirable difficulties to enhance learning', in M. A. Gernsbacher and J. Pomerantz (eds.), *Psychology and the Real World: Essays illustrating fundamental contributions to society* (2nd edn.), (pp. 59-68). New York, NY: Worth.

Jonathan Firth (2018), 'The application of spacing and interleaving approaches in the classroom', *Impact*, (2).

Christopher N. Wahlheim, John Dunlosky and Larry L. Jacoby (2011), 'Spacing enhances the learning of natural concepts: An investigation of mechanisms, metacognition, and aging', *Memory and Cognition*, 39, (5), 750–763.

▶ **Keyword search:** Spacing; spaced repetition; blocking; massing; massed practice; distributed practice; desirable difficulties; memory.

# PERSONAL REFLECTION

Have your quizzes, tests or assessments been designed to add some strategically planned spacing between your initial input and the act of recall?

What has been your previous approach to the sequencing of your lessons? Have you structured your units in a traditional 'blocked' or 'massed practice' way? Or have you used spacing to allow some time for forgetting?

With the research on spacing in mind, how might you change your classroom delivery or assessment design to utilise the power of spacing?

# CHAPTER 3

# INTERLEAVING

Interleaving is comparing and contrasting similar topics so that students can effectively identify key differences. In this chapter we will explore the research behind interleaving and why it is a more effective way to learn. We will then consider what it means for us both in the classroom and in how we design our curriculum.

# TEACHER 1.0

**1.0**

Similar to the previous chapter on spacing out our content in a more intelligent fashion, there has been relatively little attention given over the past decades to the interleaving of different topics or units to enable students to compare and contrast between them. In the past, teachers would probably have told you that the best way to understand a specific topic inside out was to give 100 per cent focus to it, so that you could master it. After all, if you're trying to learn one topic, why waste time looking at another? How could that possibly make for a more effective way to study? Students and staff alike used to tell you that the best way to learn something was to concentrate all your efforts on it. Just as we discussed in the previous chapter, 'blocking' or 'massing' your study was always thought to be the most sensible way to devote time to one topic, and greater understanding and learning were expected to be the outcomes as a result.

However, we now know that this may not be the case, especially for more advanced learners. Not only does 'blocking' or 'massing' our lesson content on one specific topic fail to give our students any time to forget this information (see Chapter 2, page 14), it also makes lessons far too easy for our more advanced learners because they don't have to use anywhere near as much brain power as they would if a different technique, topic or skill was introduced to them during this period. Historically, this approach has meant that a class would spend a whole lesson or unit studying and practising the same ideas or skills. For example, in a maths class, the students may have been looking at angles on a straight line all lesson, or alternatively, in a PE lesson, they may have been practising forehand tennis shots. But once students have focused their brain on the single topic in hand, it becomes far too easy for them, because they are not having to identify a topic by its specific features. For example, in the maths scenario, once you know that angles on a straight line add up to 180 degrees, it doesn't take that much brain power to get through the lesson, calculating the specific angles that are missing. However, if another question was posed in the form of the angles in a circle, the student would have to identify a different rule of maths and select the correct solution to solve the problem, thus using far more brain power in the process. By not knowing what is coming next, the 'desirable difficulty' levels are far greater.

The same goes for the tennis lesson. If students only ever practised forehand shots all at once in a blocked session before moving on to backhand shots the next lesson, they would know exactly what shot to play and how to stand

and hold the racket before the ball was even served to them. However, this is completely different to a game situation where the student would have to quickly and accurately identify the speed and direction of the ball coming towards them, before selecting the most effective shot to use in order to return the ball over the net.

Our failure to understand the learning benefits of using this extra brain power and the impact it has on our ability to identify something and then compare and contrast it against another example has led students to perform quite poorly when it comes to exams. Seldom do exam papers keep students in their comfort zone by asking them a block of questions on one topic before moving on to the next. In exams, students have to identify a problem (from a range of problems that they have been learning) and then select the correct solution for that problem. However, if we have never exposed our students to this skill of comparing and contrasting between different content and problems, how can we suddenly expect them to do it in examinations?

# WHAT DOES THE RESEARCH SAY?

Although the research around interleaving is usually connected to spacing, it is important to notice the distinct differences. Spacing is required in order for interleaving to be effective, but the specific research on interleaving goes much further than just linking it to retrieval practice and memory. If interleaving is implemented effectively, students will be able to truly understand the key features of a specific topic, as opposed to only being able to remember it, thus resulting in far deeper learning. In this section, we will focus on two key studies:

▶ Nate Kornell and Robert A. Bjork (2008), 'Learning concepts and categories: Is spacing the "enemy of induction"?', *Psychological Science*, 19, (6), 585–92.

▶ Doug Rohrer (2012), 'Interleaving helps students distinguish among similar concepts', *Educational Psychology Review*, 24, 355–367.

## NATE KORNELL AND ROBERT BJORK

In 2008, Nate Kornell and Robert Bjork set out to try and determine if an interleaving style of delivery is more effective for understanding and long-term learning than a blocked or massed style of delivery. In their study, they asked two groups of students to learn how to distinguish between paintings from 12 different artists who all had specific styles. The idea was to see whether they could detect the specific intricacies of what made each painting belong to a certain artist. In one group, students were exposed to the paintings of each artist in a blocked way and studied each artist one at a time, effectively mastering the style of the artist before moving on to the next. In the other group, students were given an exposure to the paintings in an interleaved way, comparing and contrasting the differences between artists once they had grasped the basic features of each artist. In the final test, students were presented with paintings in a random order and were asked to identify the artist of each painting.

Results of the study demonstrated that the group of students who had been exposed to the paintings in an interleaved way performed significantly better on the final test than the group who had studied the paintings in a blocked way. The 'blocked' practice group answered an average of 36 per cent of paintings correctly, compared to the interleaved group who answered 59 per cent correctly. This demonstrated that the fact they had to continuously discriminate between paintings throughout their period of study, and identify differences rather than just commonalities, meant that they understood the artists' styles in a far deeper way.

**Interleaving of different styles or grouping of problems lets students compare and contrast between key features.**

However, perhaps the most surprising and significant finding of the study was that, even after the test had clearly identified greater test performance via an interleaved exposure to the artists' styles, 80 per cent of the students still said that they preferred a blocked method of delivery. This raises the same issues we encountered in Chapter 2, page 18, around how 'blocked' and 'massed' delivery methods of instruction produce a false sense of fluency and confidence that students will always favour, even when it is proven to be a less effective strategy for learning. If it looks and feels better in practice because of apparent high performance, students will generally opt for that style of study over an interleaved approach that feels harder in practice but produces better long-term learning. We see this especially at home when students have free choice over their study methods. In short, what Kornell and Bjork have confirmed is that confidence will always drive behaviour when it comes to learning.

**Even though interleaving has been proven to be a more effective study method than 'blocking' or 'massed practice', students will still prefer 'blocking' due to the false sense of fluency and confidence that it brings.**

# DOUG ROHRER

In his paper, 'Interleaving helps students distinguish among similar concepts', Doug Rohrer looks more deeply into the effect of interleaving on learning. In the study, Rohrer set out to explore whether or not the improvement in learning we see is simply because of the natural spacing that is built into any effective interleaved delivery method – in his own words, 'whether the interleaving effect is a spacing effect in masquerade'. By analysing and comparing the results of a series of studies on spacing and interleaving (Kang and Pashler, 2012; Kornell and Bjork, 2008; Mitchell et al., 2008; Wahlheim et al., 2011), Rohrer was able to isolate the spacing effect from interleaving (through picking studies that had controlled for the effect of spacing). He was therefore able to come to a far more definitive judgement on whether interleaving on its own can contribute to greater gains in learning.

**By implementing interleaving, you will naturally introduce some spacing into your sequencing of lessons.**

Rohrer's interpretation of the studies found that, once spacing and interleaving had been disentangled from one another, 'interleaving per se, and not the incidental spacing that accompanies interleaving, can sharply improve learning'. His explanation confirms the conclusions of Kornell and Bjork: that interleaving makes it easier for learners to compare and contrast information in one category with information in a different category. Rohrer demonstrates this in simple terms by stating that, although items in one category may differ from the items in another category, by placing them together, the juxtaposition of the two categories enables you to clearly understand their differences.

**Interleaving per se, and not just the incidental spacing that accompanies interleaving, can sharply improve learning.**

In his summary of the evidence, Rohrer expresses caution over how schools and educational establishments should proceed with the implementation of interleaving. Many of the findings from the studies that he referenced were obtained in laboratory settings and not in classrooms. For this reason, he suggests that, until more studies are carried out in classroom conditions, schools need to be apprehensive about the wholesale endorsement of interleaving. However, what Rohrer does recommend is that, due to the benefits that have already been recorded, schools and teachers must at least use interleaving as part of a wider range of delivery methods.

# TEACHER 2.0

Now we have seen that the research has given us sufficient evidence to want to explore this further in our classrooms, let's take a look at several ways to begin interleaving your subject content to bring about deeper understanding and improved long-term learning.

## IDEA 9: INTERLEAVE RELATED CONTENT

### Similar, but not the same.

When starting out with interleaving, it is important to make sure that the content you are going to interleave is of a similar nature. One of the mistakes that lots of people make when first trying interleaving is just to mix up all of their content in a seemingly random order. This misconception is generated from people hearing that it is good to switch from topic to topic so that you keep students' brains from slipping into a comfort zone. However, the research is very clear that this is not an effective way to learn and it shouldn't be seen as just throwing all of your curriculum in the air and then teaching it in the order that it comes down. This can be extremely counterproductive for learning due to the time lost by what is called the 'task-switching cost'.

To make interleaving an effective form of delivery, content needs to be related in some way so that students can experience the true benefits of being able to compare and contrast between the content, as well as discriminating between the finer details and identifying the correct methods or solutions to solve a problem. The sequencing of lessons, or interleaving of contrasting content within a lesson, is a fine art. This may take a significant amount of time at the curriculum construction stage but, if done correctly and intelligently, can create far more fertile conditions for learning and deep understanding than a 'blocked' or 'massed' delivery method can. Try to look for topics or themes that have similar foundations or skills, so that key differences can be observed. You may find that this is best done when looking at an overview of all your topics and themes.

## IDEA 10: SOMETHING OLD, SOMETHING NEW

**Compare a previous topic or skill with the new one that you're teaching.**

Building on the previous idea of interleaving similar content, one of the best ways to do this is to compare and contrast one topic with another topic or skill that students have already learned about. Not only will students already have sufficient knowledge of the previous topic or skill so as not to make the task too difficult, it also serves to deepen their understanding on both the old and the new topic or skill, thus gaining benefits across multiple areas of your curriculum at the same time.

Depending on how desirably difficult you want to make the interleaving task and their ability to discriminate between the two areas of content, you can employ the spacing theory that we discussed in Chapter 2, page 17. The longer ago that you taught the topic you want to interleave into today's lesson, the more difficult it will be for your students to successfully compare and contrast between the intricate details. By combining these two strategies of desirable difficulty together, you are creating an extremely fertile learning environment that not only deepens understanding of the content areas, but also helps to strengthen the memory of them for future recall.

# IDEA 11: MIX AND MATCH WORKSHEETS
### *Variety is the spice of life.*

It is one thing being in control of the interleaving in your classroom because you decide which topics to interleave together, but it's another thing to try and get your students to do it independently at home. As we already know, students will always favour a 'blocked' or 'massed' study schedule of their own because of the artificial confidence and false sense of fluency that it brings. By creating your own worksheets that contain a series of questions or problems, interleaved amongst each other, it forces your students into an independent interleaved environment. These worksheets can then be used for independent study in the run-up to assessments or examinations, or potentially as part of a 'lagged homework' task (see Chapter 2, page 20).

The other benefit of creating these worksheets yourself is that you can control the level of interleaving in each worksheet. If you leave this to your students to work out, they may fall into the trap of trying to interleave topics or skills that are too different from one another, therefore not producing any real gains in learning. As the skilled teacher, you can intelligently design a series of questions that differ slightly from one another due to their design or the content that they are testing, enabling students to have to carefully identify the key differences in each problem and select the correct solution.

**TEACHING TIP**

*Why not create various levels of desirable difficulty on different worksheets? Some worksheets might include interleaved questions from recent topics and therefore might be at the easier end of the spectrum. However, you may also decide to create some more difficult worksheets, by gradually interleaving topics or skills with longer input distances between them. The same may also go for the amount of differences or commonalities between each topic. If there are only slight and subtle differences between content, it may be more difficult for students to discriminate between these fine details.*

# IDEA 12: DON'T GIVE UP
### *Nothing worth having comes easy.*

As we already know from the research by Kornell and Bjork, students will initially find this new method of delivery harder and will probably tell you that they don't like it, or that it isn't working for them. The evidence behind their gut feelings will be due to an immediate loss of confidence, stemming from lower 'performance' in the short term. However, this level of desirable difficulty is exactly what students need if they are to deepen their learning of that content. If their brains aren't being made to work hard, in order to identify, compare, contrast and discriminate, then it either becomes too easy or results in a false sense of fluency or confidence, stemming from students mistaking recognition for understanding.

The way to combat this is to be open with the students about why you are implementing interleaving and the benefits it will have on their learning. By providing students with concrete examples, like the tennis example on page 26, students can begin to see that it might make practice harder in the first instance, but if they are training their brain to work in an environment more closely aligned to what they will find in exams or in real life, this will be a far better way to increase and deepen long-term learning.

**TEACHING TIP**

*A wise man named Paul Dix once said to me that 'the school you want is only 30 days away, but people give up too early'. By committing to interleaving for at least 30 days, you can start to get past the initial concerns of students that it is harder or that they don't like it. Over the course of the month, you can make interleaving a part of your regular delivery pattern, so that students begin to get used to it and potentially even see the benefits that it yields.*

# FURTHER READING

If you want to continue your reading into the research around interleaving and its practical uses in the classroom, here are some useful starting points.

▶ **Researchers:** Nate Kornell, Robert A. Bjork, Doug Rohrer, Luke G. Eglington, Sean H. K. Kang, Monica S. Birnbaum.

▶ **Publications:** Nate Kornell and Robert A. Bjork (2008), 'Learning concepts and categories: Is spacing the "enemy of induction"?', *Psychological Science*, 19, (6), 585–92.

Doug Rohrer (2012), 'Interleaving helps students distinguish among similar concepts', *Educational Psychology Review*, 24, 355–367.

Luke G. Eglington, Sean H. K. Kang (2017), 'Interleaved presentation benefits science category learning', *Journal of Applied Research in Memory and Cognition*, 6, (4), 475–485.

Monica S. Birnbaum, Nate Kornell, Elizabeth L. Bjork and Robert A. Bjork (2013), 'Why interleaving enhances inductive learning: The roles of discrimination and retrieval', *Memory and Cognition*, 41, (3), 392–402.

▶ **Keyword search:** Interleaving; interleave; mixed practice; varied practice; blocking; massing; massed practice; distributed practice; desirable difficulties.

# PERSONAL REFLECTION

In terms of how you have previously taught your subject content, have you ever interleaved similar concepts together so that students have to compare and contrast between the subtle differences? If so, what effect has it had on learning? How did students find it?

Having now read and had the chance to reflect on the research on interleaving, how might you change your classroom delivery approach to include some aspects of interleaving?

# CHAPTER 4

# QUESTIONING

Asking effective questions is an essential part of your formative assessment to inform responsive teaching. It also provides students with opportunities for deeper thinking. In this chapter we will take a closer look at the research behind effective questioning, so that you can make the most out of one of the most important tools in our toolbox.

# TEACHER 1.0

**1.0**

Ever since the dawn of time, teachers have asked questions of their students. But thinking back to my teacher training year, I can't recall much, if any, quality training or advice I was given on how to question students effectively. Having observed hundreds of lessons in multiple schools as a senior leader, and walking in and out of classrooms on a daily basis, it is clear that I wasn't the only one who didn't get this training. Teachers in every classroom and every country across the world are asking questions, but in far too many cases with little impact on deep thinking and learning. There is a commonly held belief between educational researchers across the world that teachers ask between 300 and 400 questions per day and as many as 120 questions per hour. The most worrying thing about this is that, if conducted effectively, questioning can be one of the most powerful tools in any teacher's armoury. It's quite concerning then that we rely so much on our questioning, but spend so little time thinking about it. Without hardly any extra planning, workload or resources, questioning can be the perfect vehicle for pace, challenge, deep thinking and assessment. If we can get our teachers to question more effectively, the impact on learning will be significant.

Here are the three most common errors that Teacher 1.0 has been making in recent times. You may be able to spot some of these errors in your own or your colleagues' daily practice, or have experienced being a recipient of them as a student yourself.

## HANDS-UP QUESTIONING

If you do a Google search for the word 'teacher', you will see within the first few images several pictures of teachers standing in front of students who have their hands up, looking like they are answering questions. This has been a trademark of the teaching profession but has never done much, if anything, to promote high-quality learning in the classroom. Think back to your own days as a student in the classroom. If you knew that your teacher was always (and only ever) going to pick people with their hands up to answer questions, then you could quite quickly work out that, if you didn't want to think or participate, you just had to keep your hands down or in your pockets. Worse still, if, as a teacher, you judge whether to move on in your lesson by asking a couple of questions and getting a correct answer from one enthusiastic or knowledgeable student, then your formative assessment can hardly be classed as robust or inclusive of all students.

# WAIT TIME

Unfortunately, the very reason you ask a question is because you want an answer. So, when someone thrusts their hand in the air enthusiastically the second you've asked a question, it can be extremely tempting to take a quick answer from someone. Over time, we've seen this far too often in our classrooms. In fact, many studies have now shown that the average wait time that we give to students between asking a question and getting a response is less than one second (see for example Stahl, 1994). This presents us with many problems. Firstly, how can anyone give you their best thought-out answer in less than one second? Secondly, everyone in the class needs time to start thinking about the question that you have just posed. By taking an answer so quickly, you are depriving the vast majority of the class any time to think at all before someone gives them the answer. And thirdly, if you are one of those students who doesn't want to participate and is 'mentally truanting' or 'checking out' of the lesson by not wanting to put their hand up, then this plays right into your hands. There's no point even beginning to think about something if someone is going to do the thinking for you.

# DEEP THINKING

For effective questioning to have some impact on learning, it has to be the catalyst for deep thinking. However, students are often not pushed hard enough into thinking deeply about the questions that teachers pose every day. In the majority of cases, this can be seen when teachers are happy to accept the first answer that a student provides them with, rather than pushing and probing them to construct a much more detailed or articulate answer. In the worst cases, teachers even reword the answer that a student gives them, making it a far better answer than the student provided, telling the class that this is what they meant and praising them for their understanding. If we really want our questioning to get students to think, then we need to be prepared to probe further and further into students' minds, not letting them get away with the first thing they can tell us, but asking them to keep going, or coming back to them to extend their answer further. Think about how many times each lesson your students actually have to think deeply for themselves and in silence. Deep thinking also doesn't have to be related to a question that they will get an answer for. Some of the best thinking can happen when you pose an open-ended question that requires them to ponder something over a number of lessons.

# WHAT DOES THE RESEARCH SAY?

Like many other forms of education research that we are only just beginning to discover and see filter down to our classrooms, research on effective questioning has been around for decades but seemingly ignored by many. By getting to grips with this research and using it to positively influence our daily classroom practice, we can begin to get our students thinking far more deeply, far more frequently. The following section will explore these two studies specifically:

▶ Mary Budd Rowe (1986), 'Wait time: Slowing down may be a way of speeding up!', *Journal of Teacher Education*, 37, (1), 43–50.

▶ Paul Black and Dylan Wiliam (1998), 'Inside the black box: Raising standards through classroom assessment', *Phi Delta Kappan*, 80, (2), 139–144.

## MARY BUDD ROWE

Although Mary Budd Rowe had been researching the effects of wait time on learning and student achievement for nearly 20 years prior to her 1986 article in *The Journal of Teacher Education*, her concise summary and conclusions on the impact of wait time in the journal should have served to draw a line in the sand for all teachers. Rowe's work not only discovered the positive effect that wait time has on students, but also the impact it has on teachers, meaning that it was a pivotal summary of her research findings that we should all have been exposed to a long time ago.

Rowe identified two types of wait time – wait time 1 (the length of time given between asking a question and a student beginning to respond) and wait time 2 (the length of time given by the teacher after a student gives an answer and before the teacher begins to respond). In most cases, Rowe found that teachers were allowing less than one-second wait time between asking a question and students starting to reply. The same timeframe was also found to commonly exist between a student finishing their answer and the teacher beginning to respond.

**On average, teachers give less than one-second wait time between asking questions and taking responses.**

These observations, and Rowe's many trials and studies on providing extra wait time (both before an answer is taken and after an answer has been provided), demonstrated that just by increasing this wait time to between two and three seconds, it had a profound effect on learning as well as teacher attitudes and expectations. Rowe's article summarised a multitude of ways in which increasing wait time to approximately three seconds benefited both students and teachers. Some of the key findings are listed below.

# EFFECTS OF WAIT TIME ON STUDENTS

According to Rowe's findings, increasing wait time to three seconds has the following benefits for students:

▶ The length of student responses increases between 300 and 700 per cent. Students begin to offer far more complex and detailed explanations, rather than just short phrases. By taking the time to think first, students are far more likely to articulate their answer better, elaborating on the finer details. Students have a chance to plan and rehearse quickly what they want to say mentally, rather than just saying the first thing that comes into their head.

▶ Students listen to each other's answers more and student-to-student exchanges increase. If wait time is under one second, students just compete for turns to perform for the teacher. When wait time increases (especially after an answer is provided), students pay far more attention to what is being discussed and are happier to interact with either supportive or contrasting views.

▶ The failure of students to respond to questions significantly decreases. By providing students with sufficient wait time to think deeply about the question and recall their knowledge on the subject, students are in a far better position to answer with increased confidence.

▶ The number of students willing to participate in answering questions increases significantly. When wait time is under one second, the majority of questions are regularly responded to by a small minority of students in the class. Once you give them more time to think, more students become active participants.

 **By increasing wait time to nearly three seconds, the quality of responses increases significantly.**

# EFFECTS OF WAIT TIME ON TEACHERS

Rowe's research indicates that three seconds' wait time also has benefits for teachers:

▶ Teachers begin to ask more probing and reflective questions. This is partly down to students having more time to think about the questions, but also due to the teachers having time to consider the responses that they receive before they respond.

▶ Expectations for student responses increase. By giving more wait time, teachers begin to expect better responses. During this wait time, teachers also have time to survey the room and ask for responses from specific individuals who may not have previously participated in quick-fire questioning.

 **By increasing the wait time after an answer has been provided, teachers and students listen more attentively and are far more reflective on what has been said.**

# PAUL BLACK AND DYLAN WILIAM

In 1998, Paul Black and Dylan Wiliam wrote a paper called 'Inside the black box: Raising standards through classroom assessment', which turned out to be one of the most influential pieces of work on classroom assessment in modern times. The article formed the foundations of many studies on assessment thereafter and shed light on how to raise standards in education from within the classroom itself. Although the focus of the paper was assessment in the broader sense, teacher questioning is a key feature of formative assessment and was afforded several column inches in the paper, highlighting its importance in raising classroom standards.

Building on the work of Mary Budd Rowe a decade before them, Black and Wiliam identified that a lack of wait time resulted in most teachers' questioning being unproductive. However, they also started to connect a lack of effective wait time with a culture of students quickly raising their hand to answer questions and, more importantly, teachers only asking for responses from students with their hands up. (This led to further significant work by Dylan Wiliam in more recent years on formative assessment and questioning.) This quick-fire culture of rapid questioning meant that students who didn't want to think didn't have to because they knew that the answer, or another question, would come along almost immediately. To lots of students, this signalled that there was no point in trying in the first place. They could just sit back, leaving the answering of the questions to their few enthusiastic classmates who were always going to be able to answer more quickly than them. For many students, this also minimised the risk factor of potentially getting an answer wrong in front of their peers. A far safer strategy was simply not to participate in this guessing game.

 **If students know that their peers will probably answer before they have had a chance to think, they will give up thinking about the questions.**

This unproductive questioning was not only the catalyst for a lack of cognitive engagement from many students; Black and Wiliam also identified that it had potentially dangerous ramifications for teachers if they based their dynamic formative assessment upon it. If questioning is only actively engaging a minority of students in the classroom, then any responses you gain from them are not a good enough sample size to determine the knowledge and understanding of the whole class. Black and Wiliam found that, due to this, many teachers were out of touch with the understanding of most of the class.

 **If teachers only ask questions to a small proportion of the class, they will never be able to judge how much the majority of students have learned or understood.**

These initial findings and conclusions have prompted Dylan Wiliam to conduct a significant amount of work into formative assessment since 1998, looking at the best ways teachers can use questioning techniques and other forms of assessment effectively as part of their responsive teaching strategies.

# TEACHER 2.0

**2.0**

Now we're familiar with some of the key research in this area, let's take a look at some simple ways in which you can increase the effectiveness of your questioning, enabling you to engage students in deeper thinking opportunities and provide you with robust formative assessment.

# IDEA 13: INCREASE WAIT TIME

### *Students need time to think.*

If you recognise yourself in the research from Mary Budd Rowe because you have been guilty on far too many occasions of inviting students to respond to your questions without any significant thinking time, it is important to do something about it. Start by trying to extend the time you give your students to think by counting to three in your head, or taking a deep breath before asking for a student to respond. This will not only give students time to ponder the question and formulate a response, but it will also give you time to survey the room and choose who you want to answer the question.

One thing that will be a barrier to this strategy working is if you still allow students to put their hands up to answer questions. Even though you might give students wait time before you ask them to respond, they will probably still have thought about the answer in less than a second and raised their hand quickly to compete with their peers to be given the chance to answer the question. The chances of the student changing their answer in their head whilst waiting for you to choose them is relatively slim. The answer they thought of immediately before they raised their hand in the air will still be very similar to the answer that they give you, irrespective of any wait time that you give them.

> **TEACHING TIP**
>
> *This has to be a strategy that you commit to consistently as part of your daily classroom practice. Students need to get into the habit of not shouting out answers or raising their hands immediately. Once students are comfortable with short periods of silent thinking time, only then will deeper thinking occur. Therefore, build this into your routines and stick to it. You can't just use quick-fire, rapid-answering questioning one day and then expect students to fall back into a routine of silent wait time the day after.*

# IDEA 14: HANDS-DOWN QUESTIONING

### *I'm in charge of who will answer the questions.*

Building on wait time in the previous idea, one of the most effective classroom strategies is not to allow students to raise their hands to answer questions, unless you ask them to. By doing this, you begin to take control of who answers the questions, meaning that you start to move away from the situation that Black and Wiliam describe in their paper: when only the minority of students frequently participate. This also naturally builds in wait time as you ponder which student you are going to select to answer the question. The key here is that none of the students know which one of them will be asked to answer the question, so they all have to cognitively engage in thinking about the answer in case they are chosen.

Selecting which student answers a specific question can be dependent on a multitude of factors. You may decide to ask a student of a lower ability to start with, reflecting on their answer with some further wait time, and then ask someone of a higher ability to build on it. You may also want to include several pupil premium students in your questioning, ensuring that your formative assessment strategies probe and challenge them to think harder than they would have done normally. Alternatively, you might just want to ask the boy sat beside the window because for the last few minutes you have seen him looking out of the window and you just want to make sure that he has been paying attention.

## TEACHING TIP

*Some teachers can be drawn to online random name generators or lollipop sticks with students' names on. Although this may serve to randomise your questioning, meaning that absolutely anyone can be asked, it doesn't give you any licence to select which students you want to answer certain questions. There is a definite skill in selecting the right students at the right time to answer specific questions, and a teacher who knows their group inside out does not need a random name generator to do this for them. By completely randomising your questioning, you take away a significant proportion of the power that effective questioning can bring.*

# IDEA 15: WHOLE-CLASS RESPONSE SYSTEMS

### *3, 2, 1. Show me what you've got.*

One way of actively engaging all students in thinking about your questions and answering them is to use a range of whole-class response systems. These systems are very easy to devise and can be extremely effective to find out what everyone in the class is thinking at any point in your lesson. With a whole-class response system, everyone has to respond to the question at the same time, so, with a quick glance around the room, you can judge the knowledge and understanding of everyone – something that Black and Wiliam said was missing in the majority of questioning that they experienced in classrooms.

For questions where students have to come up with their own answer, mini-whiteboards are the best and most effective way to survey the thoughts of a whole class at the same time. Students get a specific amount of time (wait time) to think about the question and write down their answer on their board, before holding it up when the teacher asks them to. With a quick glance around the room, the teacher can see the type and range of answers from the students and ascertain their level of understanding either as individuals or as a whole class.

For questions where you may give students a choice of answers to pick from (multiple-choice questioning), you don't even need whiteboards for all students to participate. Just number your selection of answers on your main classroom whiteboard and then, after a period of designated wait time, get your students to hold up either 1, 2 or 3 fingers, depending on the answer that they have selected.

---

**TEACHING TIP** *If you are using mini-whiteboards with your students as part of your whole-class response system, you can easily use a selection of answers from students to address misconceptions and mistakes. By simply taking a selection of wrong answers and asking students to talk through why they might have come up with the answer they have or where they might have gone wrong in their thinking, you will start to deepen your class's understanding even further and move towards students working in a metacognitive fashion.*

---

# IDEA 16: SCRIPT KEY QUESTIONS

### *Plan what you want to ask rather than just opening your mouth and hoping a good question comes out.*

If we're giving students more wait time to process their thoughts before answering our questions, then we should be able to expect higher-quality answers in return. This also means that we can construct more complex questions to enable students to think far more deeply about the subject content before responding. It can be easy in the midst of a lesson to suddenly want to ask a question and, before you know it, you've opened your mouth and asked it. But if there has been no thinking time on your behalf about how to ask it, the specific language to use, and how to phrase it to get the most out of the question, then we have probably wasted a great opportunity for high-quality formative assessment. If we multiply this by the number of times we do this every lesson and every day, it's clear how many missed opportunities for deeper thinking we potentially let slip through our fingers.

By spending time planning and scripting your questions, you can ensure you use the right balance of open and closed questions in your lessons. Closed questions are great for factually right or wrong questions, but open questions can develop deeper thinking and promote far more discussion between students as they debate the finer points of an argument. Scripting your questions does not only have to be about *what* you are going to ask, but it can also involve specifically *when* in your lesson you are going to ask something and *to whom*. Rather than just hoping you ask questions at the right time, why not plan out exactly what you are going to ask and when? The question will then become a hinge question that provides you with a dynamic formative assessment of students' knowledge and understanding or that naturally leads into your next task.

**TEACHING TIP**

*Try to spend more time planning key questions for your lessons rather than feeding back on work that students have done. Your questions, if crafted carefully and effectively, will result in students doing far more deep thinking than they do when they briefly read your comments on their work. You may start to see that this is time well spent and has a far greater impact than the time you devote to marking books.*

# FURTHER READING

If you want to continue your reading into the research around questioning and its practical uses in the classroom, here are some useful starting points.

▶ **Researchers:** Mary Budd Rowe, Paul Black, Dylan Wiliam, Robert J. Stahl.

▶ **Publications:** Mary Budd Rowe (1986), 'Wait time: Slowing down may be a way of speeding up!', *Journal of Teacher Education*, 37, (1), 43–50.

Paul Black and Dylan Wiliam (1998), 'Inside the black box: Raising standards through classroom assessment', *Phi Delta Kappan*, 80, (2), 139–144.

Dylan Wiliam and Siobhan Leahy (2015), *Embedding Formative Assessment*. West Palm Beach, FL: Learning Sciences International.

Dylan Wiliam (2017a), *The Handbook for Embedded Formative Assessment*. Bloomington, IN: Solution Tree Press.

Robert J. Stahl (1994), 'Using "Think-Time" and "Wait-Time" skilfully in the classroom', *ERIC Digest*, ED370885.

▶ **Keyword search:** Questioning; wait time; deep thinking; formative assessment; responsive teaching; whole-class response systems.

# PERSONAL REFLECTION

Do you give your students sufficient wait time in order to promote deeper thinking before answering questions? If so, what techniques do you use in order to be consistent in your approach?

How do you ensure that all students are thinking when you pose a question? Do you use a 'hands-down' approach where you are in control of who answers the question? Or do you use a whole-class response system that involves all students in your class? How effective are these strategies?

Having now reflected on the research on questioning, how might you change your approach to questioning in the classroom so that you can increase the amount of deep thinking that your students have to do every lesson?

CHAPTER 5

# ASSESSMENT

Let's
be clear: this is
assessment *for* learning,
rather than just assessment *of*
learning. In this chapter we will look
at the research around assessment and
clarify the differences between formative
and summative assessment. There are
also plenty of practical ideas for how
you can begin to use assessment
as a learning tool, not just as a
measurement
tool.

# TEACHER 1.0

Just like when we talked about questioning in the previous chapter, teachers have been using assessments for hundreds of years as a means to judge how much students have actually learned of the content that has been taught. Commonly, these assessments have been in the form of written examinations or classroom tests where students answer a series of questions based on information from the topics that they have been learning. We can all probably remember the countless hours of tests and examinations that we went through, from when we first walked in the door at primary school, all the way until we left university. However, even though assessment is used so widely by so many, it is a surprisingly untapped resource when it comes to using it as a learning tool. All too often, assessment has only been used by teachers to quantify how much students have learned, and not as a vehicle to promote further learning.

Assessment has certainly always been part of Teacher 1.0's toolbox but, far too often, the following mistakes have been made, resulting in missed opportunities for learning.

## WRITING ASSESSMENTS WITHOUT MUCH THOUGHT ABOUT ASSESSMENT DESIGN

Teachers have regularly written their own tests and assessments for their students to complete. This has always seemed like a sensible thing to do because you can tailor the questions to the exact topics that you have been teaching and place them in the order that you want them. By creating it yourself, you also have the flexibility to make the assessment as short or as long as you need it to be. However, although on the face of it this might sound great, it has placed significant limitations on the learning benefits that these assessments yield.

By writing your own questions, you have no real indication of the level of difficulty that your questions pose and whether this is consistent with the previous assessment you designed or any future assessment that you design. If the questions in this assessment are constructed in a much more complex fashion than in previous assessments, then student performance might drop as a result of a lack of ability to decode the question and not due to a lack of subject knowledge. Examination boards trial and test their assessments for two to three years before they are published as standardised tests in order to ascertain a consistent level of difficulty in their questions, so that one year is not significantly harder or easier than the next. By writing your own questions the night before you get students to answer them, you can never be sure that your questions are pitched at the right level.

# USING SUMMATIVE ASSESSMENTS FOR FORMATIVE PURPOSES

Linking to the previous point, a way to avoid having to write your own questions has been to use past exam papers to assess student knowledge and progress. By doing this, teachers have been able to reduce their workload and be confident that questions have been written with the correct level of difficulty built in. However, summative assessments are intended for summative purposes and are specifically designed to produce a score, grade or rank that is consistent for everyone who takes that assessment. In many ways, this has been the fuel that has fed our love (or hate) for data-tracking systems, with all meaningful assessments seemingly having to generate some form of data. Summative assessments do this very easily, but they fail when it comes to accurately identifying the reasons why students can't do something. This has also led to an unhealthy obsession with providing students in examination years (Year 6 and Year 11) with a continuous stream of past exam papers in the hope that, simply by getting students to practise question after question, their knowledge and understanding of the relevant topics will increase as a result.

# SEEING ASSESSMENT ONLY AS A WAY OF POPULATING SPREADSHEETS WITH DATA

Previously, teachers used to fill out their mark book religiously with scores from every assessment so that they had a record of how each student had performed in these tests. In more recent times, teachers now enter data into formatted spreadsheets that colour code students based on whether they have met or are working towards their target grades. This serves a useful purpose to an extent; however, as our infatuation with student performance data has increased, our intentions behind designing and setting assessments have moved even further away from them being used as a learning tool in their own right.

Far too often, teachers schedule an assessment because of an upcoming data drop on the school calendar and not because it will be the right time pedagogically to ascertain some vital information from the students that will influence responsive teaching methods. More worryingly, in many cases once the data has been entered into the spreadsheet or mark book, nothing different happens in the classroom. This is usually the case because assessments have been commonly administered at the end of a topic or unit of work to judge how much has been learned or understood. Irrespective of how well or poorly students perform, the teacher will be moving on to the next unit anyway, so the scores that the assessment generates are purely for tracking purposes and not to inform the teacher how to adjust their forthcoming plans based on the gaps in knowledge that the assessment has exposed.

## IDENTIFYING MISTAKES RATHER THAN MISCONCEPTIONS

Teachers have been the masters of identifying mistakes in assessments, but rarely have these tests been used to identify misconceptions. If our assessments only identify that students have got something right or wrong, then we will never be in a position to know whether a student has just made a mistake or has forgotten the information – or more importantly, whether they are holding a deep-seated misconception about something. If a student has a deep-seated misconception about something, it doesn't matter how many times you assess them on it – unless you address that misconception, they will always get that question wrong.

In the majority of assessments, misconceptions are seldom identified, meaning that the information we have been gleaning from these assessments has been at a very basic level. A student going from 70 per cent to 40 per cent in your mark book or spreadsheet means very little apart from giving a basic indication that this student has suddenly and significantly dipped in performance. If all you look at is which questions a student got right and wrong, and your questions are not designed to inform you *why* they got something wrong, then the data you collect will just serve to create pretty colour-coded spreadsheets and graphs, rather than giving you the information you require in order to shape what you do next in the classroom.

# WHAT DOES THE RESEARCH SAY?

Unlike the research in some other areas that we have explored already in this book, the vast majority of research on effective and intelligent use of assessment in schools is relatively recent. This is good news for teachers, because it means that the environment in which the research has been conducted and written about still mirrors the environment in which we currently teach, thus making it even more relevant to the classrooms of today. In this section, we will consider the following works:

▶ Dylan Wiliam (2009), 'Assessment for learning: Why, what and how? An inaugural professorial lecture'. London: UCL IOE Press.

▶ Daisy Christodoulou (2017), *Making Good Progress? The future of assessment for learning*. Oxford: Oxford University Press.

## DYLAN WILIAM

In his 2009 inaugural professorial lecture, Dylan Wiliam addressed the fact that we need to invest far more time and energy into formative assessment if we are serious about wanting to improve learning. In more recent years, through Wiliam's continued and substantial work on assessment, he makes the claim that he wished he'd renamed the term 'formative assessment' as 'responsive teaching', because the word 'assessment' conjures up a whole host of connections with tests and exams and very little about what happens next in the classroom. Wiliam feels that this may have been, in part, why the majority of assessment we still see in the classroom is assessment of learning and not assessment for learning. Teachers frequently assess students and record data in order to try to help students improve, but very little of that data ever gets acted on to change the direction of teaching in the classroom.

 **Assessment *for* learning is a very different process from assessment *of* learning.**

Wiliam simplifies this issue by asking teachers to think about the intention behind their assessment. If teachers are designing and conducting assessments in order to improve their teaching, then that falls into the 'assessment for learning' category. However, if the intention behind a teacher's assessment is to be able to grade, score or rank students on the basis of test performance, then that is 'assessment of learning'. Wiliam says that, although most teachers claim that they are assessing for learning, his research shows that he has seen plenty of formative intentions but very few formative actions. These observations prompt Wiliam to say in his lecture that 'assessment for learning becomes formative assessment only when the evidence of student learning is actually used to adapt the teaching work to meet student learning needs. If you're not using the evidence to do something that you couldn't have done without the evidence, you're not doing formative assessment'.

Once the intention behind the assessment has been established, and teaching will potentially change or be adjusted as a result of the data that the assessment provides, the timing of these changes is key. In many school systems, Wiliam has observed well-intended systems of formative assessment that work on long- or medium-term cycles, where areas of weakness are restudied before exams, or gaps in knowledge are addressed at the end of specific units of work. However, these systems usually produce very little impact on learning because misconceptions and mistakes have been left with students for too long. In Wiliam's view, formative assessment needs to be used in a short-term or immediate cycle if you want to get the most out of it. His lecture makes the point that 'if you are not using information to make a difference to your teaching within a day or two then it is unlikely to make a difference to student achievement'. In short, what Wiliam is saying is that what really matters when it comes to formative assessment in our classrooms is what happens minute by minute and day by day.

 **If all your assessment does is tell you what students can or can't do, then you'll never know _why_ they can't do it.**

## DAISY CHRISTODOULOU

Building on the foundations that Dylan Wiliam laid around the effective use of formative assessment, Daisy Christodoulou has worked alongside him to provide even further clarity on the use of assessment for learning. In her 2017 book, _Making Good Progress?_, Christodoulou offers a narrative exploring why assessment for learning hasn't transformed our schools. She also pinpoints several traps that teachers have commonly fallen into and ways to either climb out of those traps or avoid them in the first place. One of Christodoulou's key messages relates to how teachers can make better inferences on learning from their assessments, but we will return to this in Chapter 7 on 'Learning versus performance', page 77.

Focusing solely on the use of assessment for now, three key areas that Christodoulou discusses are assessment design, assessment data, and formative and summative assessments. Let's look at each of these in turn.

# ASSESSMENT DESIGN

One of the many reasons why students sometimes don't perform in line with their potential in our assessments is due to the complexity of question design. Christodoulou is quick to identify that the more difficult the wording of a question (or the inclusion of unfamiliar vocabulary), the more likely it is that a student will fail the assessment for reasons that have nothing to do with their skill in that subject. The likelihood of this happening is far greater for students with a lower ability in reading and decoding text. Therefore, a student's inability to fluently decode what the question is actually asking will mask the reasons why they might get something wrong.

The problem with this for teachers is that the errors those students make on their assessments might look the same as the errors that students who have poor subject knowledge are making. Christodoulou suggests that, in most cases, designing more complex assessments, or questions that are worded in more complex ways, means students with higher literacy skills will usually get better results. This also means that the more complex our assessments, the less useful they are as formative assessments, because they are not providing teachers with the accurate and diagnostic information they need in order to adapt their teaching accordingly.

# ASSESSMENT DATA

Just as Dylan Wiliam had inferred previously, Christodoulou suggests that one of the biggest missed opportunities when using assessments is that too many people are solely interested in the grades, levels or percentages that these assessments generate, rather than paying more attention to the exact questions that students get wrong. Christodoulou also states that this is compounded even further by a culture of accountability that requires teachers to provide numerical evidence of short- and medium-term progress between assessments. In lots of cases, this leads to teachers teaching to the test in order to prove that assessment data is heading in the right direction and showing a continuously upward trend in trying to meet student targets. Unfortunately, this can create misleading short-term gains in student performance that are mistaken for real progress and learning. In schools where this is the case, Christodoulou suggests that you usually find that the frequency of assessments is driven not by student need but by this culture of accountability. Christodoulou believes it is this culture that has been the driver for grades and levels being both misused and overused in schools all over the world in recent times.

**Far too often, assessment is focused on the data it produces and not what happens next in the classroom. A desire for regular assessment data has encouraged teaching to the test and misleading short-term gains in student performance.**

# FORMATIVE AND SUMMATIVE ASSESSMENTS

A great extension of Dylan Wiliam's work, Christodoulou's book offers a deep understanding of the differences between formative and summative assessments, together with advice on when and why you should elect to use each one as part of your assessment strategies. As Christodoulou points out, even though many teachers would tell you otherwise, there has been a lack of understanding in the teaching profession about the differences between these two assessment methods. This is highlighted by the fact that frequently an assessment designed for one particular purpose (e.g. a summative purpose) is used for a different purpose (e.g. a formative purpose).

**A lack of understanding in the role of both formative and summative assessments has resulted in many teachers trying to use summative assessments for formative purposes.**

What Christodoulou tells us quite clearly is that, irrespective of the design quality of each assessment, a great formative assessment may not be so great for summative purposes and vice versa. The more summative your assessment is in design, the blunter it is as a formative instrument to infer learning and progress. Designing an assessment for summative purposes – to generate levels and grades – has significant limitations and restrictions, meaning the assessment becomes less formative in its use. If teachers try to design an assessment that fits both needs, it can be relatively ineffective for either purpose.

# TEACHER 2.0

Now that we are familiar with some of the recent research on assessment and its use in the classroom, let's take a look at some easy-to-implement strategies so that you can make the most out of any assessment that you design.

## IDEA 17: PRE-ASSESSMENT

### Find out what they know before you start teaching them.

A common error that teachers make is holding an assumption that, just because you haven't taught them a topic yet, students will have no prior knowledge of it. In many cases, this can prove to be wrong, and significant time is wasted teaching the first couple of lessons of a topic that perhaps aren't required. By designing and conducting a pre-assessment with your students at the start of every topic, you can ascertain their level of prior knowledge and where to begin pitching your teaching. You may find that you can start from the second or third lesson, saving you significant time that you can invest elsewhere, or you may find that you need to start at Lesson –1 because of a significant lack of foundation knowledge.

There is also a surprising but significant benefit to pre-assessments. Students are being asked questions on areas that they may not have been taught before; this creates inquisition from students and lays the foundation for deeper learning. Students naturally begin to look out for the answers to the questions that they couldn't originally answer, so when they hear something that answers that original question, it becomes more significant. If the same assessment is administered at the end of the unit of work, students can also clearly identify how much they have progressed since the beginning of the topic and where there are still gaps in their knowledge.

> **TEACHING TIP**
> *Make sure you spend time discussing your intentions behind the pre-assessment so that your students aren't confused by sitting a test about a topic or unit that they have not yet been taught. Failure to talk through your strategy and how it will benefit both your delivery and their own learning can mean that students feel anxious or have their confidence significantly dented by low scores on the test.*

# IDEA 18: STOP USING SUMMATIVE ASSESSMENTS FOR FORMATIVE PURPOSES

### Don't try to fit a square peg into a round hole.

As we've seen in the research from Daisy Christodoulou, summative assessments are designed specifically to convey a shared meaning, by some form of numerical grade, to all who sit the assessment. They are not designed to identify why students can't do a certain skill or answer a specific question. By using a summative assessment in this way, you will be able to rank all of your students, based on their performance at that time, but it will provide you with little information about whether or not students actually deeply understand the content, as opposed to whether they have just got something right or wrong.

Formative assessments don't have to be scheduled as written tests at the end of a unit. In some of the most effective cases, formative assessment is an ongoing process that happens every lesson, every day. As Dylan Wiliam points out, if your formative assessment doesn't lead to you changing your teaching within a day or two, then it is probably not formative. This means that some of the questioning strategies and techniques that we discussed in Chapter 4, page 35, are great examples of daily formative assessment that should be the catalyst for adapting your teaching either within the lesson or the very next lesson. Try to establish formative assessment as part of your daily or weekly classroom routines, so that you can accurately and regularly assess what the students have learned. Whether you use verbal questioning, low-stakes quizzing, discussions or written exercises, you just need to make sure that you do something as a result of the information you gather. Simply carrying on with your short-, medium- or long-term plan regardless means that you wasted everyone's time in carrying out your formative assessment in the first place.

**TEACHING TIP**

*Before you set out to perform any form of assessment, take some time to think about your intentions and what you want to achieve. Is it simply to help you generate a progress score for an upcoming data drop? Or is it to help improve your teaching so that you can cater for the needs of your students in a far more responsive and effective way? Once you have done this, you will be in a far better place to determine which type of assessment to design and conduct with your students.*

# IDEA 19: MULTIPLE-CHOICE QUESTIONS

### *A, B, C or D… take your pick.*

There once was a time when multiple-choice questions were seen as lazy teaching. Students could simply guess the answers from a selection of options and, if they were lucky, they would get more right than they got wrong. However, in recent times, research has begun to show how we can use multiple-choice questions to identify misconceptions in learning as well as mistakes. This is a key feature of formative assessment because the difference between a student making a simple mistake and holding a deep-seated misconception is huge. If a student just makes a mistake, or has forgotten something, the chances are that in the future they may get this answer right. However, if a student is holding a misconception about something, they will get that answer wrong until the day they die, unless that misconception is addressed and corrected.

By designing a question that has three or four possible answers (via intelligent construction of the possible answers), it is possible to differentiate between a mistake and a misconception. The way to do this is to provide one correct answer, an obvious mistake, plus one or two of the common misconceptions that students usually have in this area of the topic. This way, depending on how students answer the question and which answer they decide to pick, it will give you far more insight into their knowledge and thinking on the question. If your questions identify mistakes, then a process of further practice and focus could remedy this. However, if your questions identify a series of misconceptions, then you need to address these through your teaching as soon as possible.

> **TEACHING TIP**
> *By combining Idea 15 (on whole-class response systems, page 43) with this one, you don't have to set up long written tests to establish a culture of multiple-choice questioning. By simply asking a question and providing three or four different answers on the board, students can raise the necessary number of fingers that correspond to the answer they are selecting. Using a quicker and easier method of multiple-choice questioning such as this enables you to be far more responsive to misconceptions, in a far more timely fashion.*

# IDEA 20: EXIT TICKETS

*Before you leave, show me what you've understood from today's lesson.*

If you really want to be responsive to the needs of your students and plan or tweak your next lesson according to how well students got on in today's lesson, then exit tickets are a very simple but effective way to do this. The idea is to pose a key question that relates to the main topic that you have just taught and it may be one of the most important things that you want students to understand or know. By using this as part of your plenary, students have to write their answer down on a slip of paper that you provide and hand it in before they leave the lesson. This way, the information you receive from every individual will help you judge how successfully the main information has been understood and whether you need to adjust your plans moving forward.

In terms of how you design the question, you may want to just pose a question and let students respond with their own answer, or you may want to combine the previous idea with this and use a multiple-choice question that has several answers to choose from. Just as in the previous idea, by using this method, you should also be able to identify misconceptions as well as mistakes. However, the important feature of either method is that you are not marking or grading the answers. They are purely for the formative purpose of helping you plan your future teaching. You may decide to tell students the answer to the question at the beginning of the next lesson, but there is no need to religiously hand back all of their answers and tell people if they got it right or wrong. The fact that students have had to think about and recall the information, together with you now having an indication of the level of understanding of what you have just taught, is enough.

**TEACHING TIP**

*Have some pre-cut slips of paper that students can use to answer your question. These don't need to be fancy or designed in a certain way, but can just be small slips of paper that students can write their name and answer on. If you have a pile of these pre-cut and on your desk, there is a far greater chance of you using them and handing them out at the end of a lesson, rather than having to try to find some suitable paper or the students having to hand in their books or tear pages out of their books.*

# FURTHER READING

If you want to continue your reading into the research around assessment and its practical uses in the classroom, here are some useful starting points.

▶ **Researchers:** Paul Black and Dylan Wiliam, Daisy Christodoulou, Nate Kornell, Matthew Jensen Hays, Robert A. Bjork, Nikki Booth.

▶ **Publications:** Dylan Wiliam (2009), 'Assessment for learning: Why, what and how? An inaugural professorial lecture'. London: UCL IOE Press.

Daisy Christodoulou (2017), *Making Good Progress? The future of assessment for learning.* Oxford: Oxford University Press.

Nate Kornell, Matthew Jensen Hays, and Robert A. Bjork (2009), 'Unsuccessful retrieval attempts enhance subsequent learning', *Journal of Experimental Psychology: Learning, Memory, and Cognition,* 35, (4), 989–998.

Nikki Booth (2017), 'What is formative assessment, why hasn't it worked in schools, and how can we make it better in the classroom?', *Impact,* (1).

▶ **Keyword search:** Assessment; formative assessment; summative assessment; diagnostic assessments; responsive teaching; multiple-choice questioning.

# PERSONAL REFLECTION

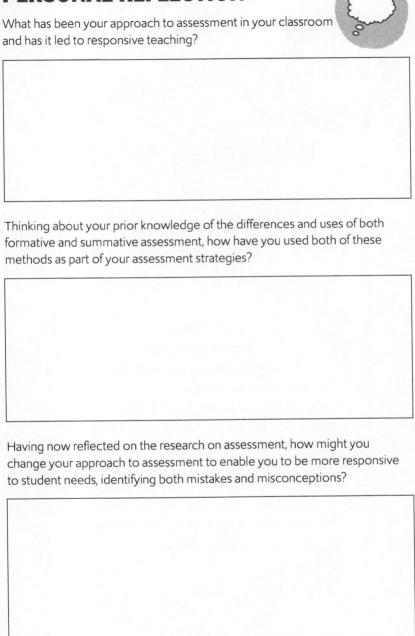

What has been your approach to assessment in your classroom and has it led to responsive teaching?

Thinking about your prior knowledge of the differences and uses of both formative and summative assessment, how have you used both of these methods as part of your assessment strategies?

Having now reflected on the research on assessment, how might you change your approach to assessment to enable you to be more responsive to student needs, identifying both mistakes and misconceptions?

# CHAPTER 6

# FEEDBACK

Feedback
is any information
that teachers give students
about their work that enables them
to reflect and make positive changes to
that piece of work or future pieces of work.
In this chapter we will look at how we may
have misinterpreted what the research has
said about feedback, along with how we
can start to use it more effectively
and efficiently without increasing
our workload.

# TEACHER 1.0

**1.0**

Ever since the dawn of time, teachers have been providing feedback to students on their work. Whether this has been in the form of ticks, percentages, grades, comments or smiley faces, our children have been given some level of feedback to tell them how well they have done or not done on a piece of work, and in some cases what they can do to improve this work further. Every teacher's essential companion has been a red pen; as a profession, we've probably kept sellers of red pens in business over the years. The way that feedback has been provided to students in our classrooms has certainly evolved over time, but in lots of cases, feedback has simply been 'marking'. This has meant that students were only told how well they had done on a specific piece of work but not asked to reflect on and improve their work further. When we look at the research on effective feedback in this chapter, we will begin to see just how important this is.

But first, let's take a deeper look at how marking and feedback have evolved over time, focusing on some of the things to which Teacher 1.0 has been devoting considerable time and effort, without much impact on student outcomes.

## TICK AND FLICK MARKING

In the past, covering a student's book with red pen was always the gold standard in demonstrating that you had taken the time to read their work and acknowledge their effort. A quick two-second glance over a page of work followed by a customary big red tick or a smiley face let the student, parent and, unfortunately more importantly, the senior leadership team know that you had fulfilled your expectations of 'marking' books within a specific timeframe. Think back to your own days at school and you'll certainly recognise this. But what impact did this ever have on student outcomes? Did the hours of taking books home for 'ticking and flicking' whilst having one eye on the television make any difference to those students, apart from the fact that they knew you had looked at their work? Did random comments like 'good work', 'great effort' or 'good boy' make any difference in the grand scheme of raising achievement?

## DETAILED COMMENTS

The first indication of an evolution in feedback came when teachers began to have to write detailed comments about the work that students had done, rather than just a tick-and-flick approach. The education profession had, at long last, begun to understand that ticking and flicking served no purpose other than to acknowledge a student's work. Once teachers had grasped the fact that the true purpose of feedback was not just to tell someone how well they had done, but to inform them how to improve further, long paragraphs of red text began to appear in students' books. This quickly became the new gold standard for teachers, and senior leaders across the country began to conduct book scrutinies, looking at the quality and frequency of comments in students' books. This was a significant increase in teachers' workload and, in many cases, teachers were putting more red pen on the book than the student had written in the first place. This culture of marking began to take hold of the profession, with teachers beginning to buy trolleys and crates on wheels to take several sets of books home at weekends, so they could spend hours and hours writing all over students' books in the hope that it would either somehow improve outcomes or impress the senior leadership team.

# GRADING WORK

Once the target- and data-driven culture that we now live in took off, teachers were then required to start frequently grading assessments and homework tasks in order to track the progress of their students and feed the spreadsheet analytics and pretty graphs that were regularly produced by school data teams. Detailed comments were soon accompanied by GCSE grades, effort grades or, in some cases, coded grading systems that only the teachers could fathom. These grades then had to be transferred into teacher mark books, spreadsheets and tracking systems, meaning more work for the teachers even after the work had been marked. Students were all issued with target grades so that teachers, students and parents could all see if a piece of work was below the expected standard, above the expected standard or if the student had simply met their target. Teacher workload aside, this presented another problem: what motivation was there for someone who could still have made significant improvements to their work, but who had been graded at their target grade? For lots of lazy kids, this meant 'job done'.

# DEDICATED IMPROVEMENT TIME

The next stage in the evolution of feedback was not just to provide detailed comments on student work, but to ensure that comments directed students to do something to improve their work. To begin with, students were reading the comments but not necessarily doing anything about the feedback, so many schools started to dedicate some time in the next lesson to get students to improve that specific piece of work, based on the comments that the teachers had provided.

This meant that feedback was being used not just to inform students about how they had performed but, more importantly, give them some direction as to how to make their work better. This culture of feedback began to dominate teachers' lives, with some schools insisting that every piece of work needed to be marked and feedback given to students in order for them to improve. Work scrutinies by senior leaders became far more frequent, and teachers started to pride themselves and their books on the quality and length of comments that they were providing to help students improve their work.

# TRIPLE MARKING

With students now acting on feedback and improving their work, this created another problem for teachers. Did that new and improved piece of work need to be marked as well? Unfortunately, many schools said yes, meaning that the original piece of work that the student did once now needed three responses: firstly from the teacher, to recognise the areas that the student did well (known as 'what went well') and what they could do to improve ('even better if'); secondly from the student, who needed to respond to these comments and act on this feedback (sometimes in another colour or in a colour-coded box); thirdly from the teacher again, who had to mark the work to determine whether the student had actually improved it. This process clearly increased the amount of time spent on that one piece of work but, more significantly, nearly doubled the amount of marking time that teachers were having to complete. For some teachers, it was a never-ending process. What if the student hadn't made improvements after they acted on the original feedback or had made further mistakes? Should the teacher provide more detailed comments that then had to be acted on and remarked? Where and when did you stop?

At every stage of this evolution of feedback from tick and flick to triple marking, a teacher's weekly workload has significantly increased, with many teachers regularly having to spend several hours per night and at weekends marking books and providing specific feedback just to keep on top of the demands that their school has placed on them. This excessive increase in workload has been cited as one of the main factors for teachers leaving the profession. In 2019, the National Education Union ran a survey with recently qualified teachers about teacher workload. It produced some startling statistics. The survey found that 26 per cent of respondents with less than five years' teaching experience planned to quit the profession by 2024. Even 15 per cent of teachers who had only just begun their career and had less than two years' experience planned to leave the profession within this timeframe. When asked why this was, 62 per cent of all respondents cited 'out-of-control' workload pressures as one of the main reasons they had decided to try to 'get out before the job kills me'.

What is most concerning about this evolution of feedback, the excessive workload it has created and the number of teachers it has driven from the profession is that little of it has any impact on student achievement whatsoever.

# WHAT DOES THE RESEARCH SAY?

As the evolution of feedback has gathered pace, so too has the research on it. However, what is quite concerning is how little of this research is embedded in day-to-day practice in schools across the world. Teachers are still spending significant amounts of time providing feedback that either has little or no impact or, worse still, is actually damaging to the student.

Before we look at two great examples of the research on feedback, it's interesting to note that certain pieces of research in this area have made educational headlines but have been misunderstood and misinterpreted for years. Both John Hattie's work on 'feedback' through his *Visible Learning* programmes (Hattie and Clarke, 2018) and the *Sutton Trust-EEF Teaching and Learning Toolkit* (Education Endowment Foundation, 2012) consider feedback to be one of the top strategies for raising student achievement. However, in many quarters over the past decade, the word 'feedback' has been interpreted by the education profession as meaning 'marking', hence why the evolution of feedback that I described above has led us to a place of excessive workload for teachers, with little to show for it apart from a stressed-out workforce. If we really want to reboot our teaching, it is imperative to truly understand what the research says about feedback and how we can use this effectively and efficiently to raise achievement.

▶ Dylan Wiliam (2011), *Embedded Formative Assessment*. Bloomington, IN: Solution Tree Press.

▶ Alfie Kohn (2011), 'The case against grades', *Counterpoints*, 451, 143–153.

# DYLAN WILIAM

Wiliam's (2011) book *Embedded Formative Assessment* has provided us with a hugely significant insight into effective feedback and has been a catalyst for many other pieces of research and published books over the past decade. Not only did the book shine a light on how to ensure your feedback is as effective as possible, but it also demonstrated that not all feedback is good feedback and, worryingly, by providing it in the wrong way, it can actually be counterproductive and lower student performance. This is very concerning, especially given the number of hours that teachers continue to put into feeding back on student work every week. In his book, Wiliam provides the following highlights on the best ways to provide effective feedback and avoid it being counterproductive.

## THE ROLE OF FEEDBACK

Feedback is a key part of the formative assessment process, but only if it is acted on by students to improve their performance in the future. As Wiliam highlights, students require time to actually use the feedback to improve their work, so one of his key recommendations is to set aside some time in lessons to enable students to do just that. Wiliam says quite categorically that 'you should never ever give feedback unless you make the time for students to respond to it' and that 'the only thing important about feedback is what students do with it'.

 **'You should never ever give feedback unless you make the time for students to respond to it' (Wiliam, 2011). The only thing important about feedback is what students do with it.**

Wiliam (2016) has since made it clear that we need to be very careful about our intentions behind the feedback that we provide to students; it should intend to improve the student and not just the piece of work. He says that 'if feedback is too specific to the task that students have just done, they are not going to be able to apply it to a different task'. It must therefore cause students to reflect on their work and think about how they can improve their performance in the future. And it shouldn't just be thinking; something must happen as a result of the feedback. Wiliam says that 'feedback should be more work for the recipient than the donor'.

'If feedback is too specific to the task that students have just done, they are not going to be able to apply it to a different task.' (Wiliam, 2011)

 'Feedback should be more work for the recipient than the donor.' (Wiliam, 2011)

## SCORES AND COMMENTS

Wiliam points out quite clearly that students who are provided with constructive feedback (i.e. suggestions on how to improve) learn twice as fast as their peers who only receive a score on a piece of work. In his research, students who only received scores did not improve much, if at all, from task to task. However, the really interesting finding of Wiliam's research came when students were given both a score and a set of constructive comments. In this scenario, students still did not make any improvement from task to task, meaning that the score had effectively wiped out any positive benefit gained from the constructive comments. Wiliam blames this counterproductive effect on the fact that students will only focus on the numbers or letters that they receive on a piece of work and are immediately uninterested in what the comments say. Wiliam says that 'teachers who spend time crafting helpful comments are wasting their time if they also give a mark'. For students who gain high scores, why do they need to read the comments on how to improve? For students who have matched their target grade, why go the extra mile to improve their work if they have already produced work in line with their expectations? And lastly, for students who scored low marks, they simply don't want to read what they perceive to be negative comments about their work.

 Teachers who spend time crafting helpful comments are wasting their time if they also give a mark.

## UNINTENDED CONSEQUENCES

Although the intention of every teacher who provides feedback on student work is to help raise attainment, Wiliam points out that there can be unintended consequences that make the feedback counterproductive. When feedback indicates to a student that they have fallen below the desired target, there are three common responses, all of which result in the feedback having a negative effect on their future performance.

▶ The student changes their perception of the goal that they can eventually reach and begins to settle for a lower standard because that is all they feel they are capable of achieving.

▶ The student is disillusioned with the whole process and abandons their pursuit of meeting or exceeding their target grade by simply declaring that they are no good at that subject, so why bother trying?

▶ The student may not agree with the constructive criticism, in which case this may lead to a negative attitude or relationship between the student and the teacher or subject.

Only when a student takes on board this feedback and vows to make changes to their future performance will the feedback have the desired impact. Wiliam states that in most cases this only happens when students have a desire to receive feedback and believe that they will improve as a result of receiving it.

## ALFIE KOHN

In 2011, Alfie Kohn wrote a summary paper on the evidence behind the case against using grades when providing feedback on student work. While this may be an eye-opener for many in the profession, this isn't new research. Kohn cites evidence and research trials in his summary from every decade since the 1930s up to the present day, all reporting on the negative effects that grading can have on learning. Although Kohn makes the point that research on the effects of grading has slowed down in the last couple of decades, it is clear that the studies that have recently been conducted still reinforce the evidence from earlier studies and do not contradict their significant conclusions. This is another concrete example of how the research and evidence behind teaching have always been available to us but, as a profession, we have either not known of its existence, chosen not to listen to it or have made little progress in using it.

Kohn cites a range of studies that have compared students who are led to focus on grades with those who aren't. Their results all support the following conclusions:

▶ Grades tend to reduce students' real interest in whatever they are learning. A 'grading orientation' and a 'learning orientation' have been shown to be inversely related and every study that has ever investigated the impact of receiving grades on intrinsic motivation, or that emphasises the importance of getting good grades, has found a negative effect on long-term learning.

▶ Grades create a preference for students to pick the easiest possible task or the easiest route to their goal. If we impress upon students that what they are doing will count towards their grade, their response will likely be to avoid taking any unnecessary intellectual risks along the way. They will do everything they can in order to minimise the chance of doing poorly – not because they are unmotivated, but because they are being rational. They are responding to teachers who, by telling them the goal is to get a good mark, have sent the message that success matters more than learning.

▶ Grades tend to reduce the quality of students' deep thinking. They may skim books for what they need to know, rather than reading around the subject for deep knowledge. Rather than becoming inquisitive learners who are enjoying their learning, they are more likely to be asking themselves, 'Is this going to be on the test?'

▶ Grades, even when accompanied by constructive comments, promote a fear of failure even in high-achieving students and, as a result, many grade-orientated environments are associated with increased levels of cheating. Where there is a fear of failure related to specific targets, people will sometimes do whatever it takes not to fail and may compromise their own morals to get there.

▶ It is not enough just to add narrative comments to accompany grades. When comments and grades coexist, the comments are written to justify the grade. Teachers report that students often turn to the grade and ignore the comment but, when there is only a comment, they read it. Therefore, constructive comments and narratives are only helpful in the absence of grades.

 **Grade-orientated environments promote a fear of failure. Grades tend to reduce the quality of students' deep thinking and real interest in what they are learning. They motivate students only to learn for the test.**

Kohn also points out that, although some teachers and schools will feel they are starting to edge away from a grade-orientated environment due to the profession's move towards 'life without levels', there are still the underlying intentions of grading that are holding this back from being a truly transformative process. If you are simply replacing numbers or letters with statements like 'exceeding expectations' or 'meeting expectations', then you are still grading students.

# TEACHER 2.0

Now that we have got to grips with what the research is saying about how to use feedback effectively and not produce counterproductive results, let's take a look at some strategies that you can put into practice.

## IDEA 21: WHOLE-CLASS FEEDBACK

*How did we do as a class? What do we need to work on next as part of my responsive teaching?*

The biggest issue with the evolution of feedback has been the excessive workload that this has placed upon teachers. If student work suddenly needs to have detailed constructive comments on how to improve, then this adds an enormous amount of time to a teacher's working week. Students quite frequently make the same mistakes as their peers, so teachers can end up writing the same comments over and over again on lots of students' books. Due to the time it takes teachers to complete this process, even for just one piece of work (on top of their already busy schedules and lives outside of school), feedback is not always timely because it can take more than one marking session. If you see your class again before they receive their feedback, the feedback is not as useful as it would have been if it had been received the very next lesson.

With a whole-class feedback method, you review student work and create a list of common strengths and weaknesses without writing much, if anything, on individual student books. Your overview may contain sections such as: 'Areas of secure understanding', 'Next teaching steps', 'Causes for concern' and 'Star students'. This overview can be provided to students and, more importantly, can be used as a catalyst for your responsive teaching. By saving significant time by not writing detailed comments on every piece of work, you are instead enabling your feedback to be far more timely and responsive the very next lesson. Your summary sheet is also an excellent reflection document for you to gain a quick overview of the commonalities and individual areas for development, something that would have taken a significant amount of time to amass if you had to comment on every individual book.

## IDEA 22: FEEDFORWARD NOT FEEDBACK

**We need to improve the student in the future, not just the piece of work in the past.**

One of the key points that Dylan Wiliam makes is that, if feedback is too specific to the task that students have just done, they are not going to be able to apply it to a different task. The common error that most teachers make with feedback is that it is focused on improving a specific piece of work that a student has already done and not how the student can improve themselves in future pieces of work. How many times have you seen a student make the corrections that you have asked them to make, but then make exactly the same errors in a future piece of work? The student may have been compliant in responding to feedback on a specific task but has not had the chance to use this advice on a future piece of work.

Whether you are still providing individual feedback or have moved to whole-class feedback as in the previous idea, you can get students to write out what their main improvement points were at the top of their page before they begin a future piece of work. This way, they are using their feedback and the advice you are providing them with to better themselves on a future piece of work. With you feeding forwards on a future piece of work and not backwards on a previous piece of work, students are more likely to be motivated to use your comments to improve. This is much more appealing than having to go back and improve something that they already regard as finished. Most students will tell you that they aren't particularly motivated to go back over their old work and would much rather put it into practice on a new piece of work.

## IDEA 23: NO MORE GRADING

**Let students focus on what they need to improve, not how you have measured their performance.**

As the research has already stated, grading work with letters, numbers or statements can be counterproductive to long-term learning. Even when grades accompany constructive comments, they wipe out any positive effect that the comments may have. If you really want students to focus on deep learning and understanding of a topic, you need to get them to stop focusing on the grades and their 'performance' on any given task. If you can work towards students having a desire to know how they can always do better, rather than just how they have done compared to everyone else, then and only then can you begin to use feedback to its full potential.

For most formative assessments that you complete, a grade or mark is not required; it is just something that we have got into the habit of doing. The only time you may need to provide a grade is when you are required to complete a whole-school data capture. If you start to think about the intention behind your feedback and what you want it to achieve, things then become quite simple. Do you want to measure how well a student has done? Or do you want to tell a student how to improve further? By focusing on qualitative summaries of student work (either individual or whole class), you can change the narrative around formative assessments and build a culture of deep learning, rather than a fear of failure.

# IDEA 24: HYPERCORRECTION EFFECT

*It is more beneficial to uncover your own misconceptions, rather than someone doing it for you.*

In his more recent work on formative assessment and feedback, Dylan Wiliam (quoted in Hendrick and Macpherson, 2017) outlines how powerful it can be to discover your own mistakes and misconceptions, rather than somebody else doing this for you via written feedback. Finding out our own mistakes has a much greater impact on us than someone else telling us what these mistakes are. Some students, as we have seen in the research (see page 66), may dismiss feedback that is given to them by a supposed expert but, when they uncover something by themselves, it usually sticks with them. The impact of this increases in relation to how strongly you believed something to be right in the first place. You can sometimes almost not believe something is true if someone else tries to modify a strong belief that you hold, however wrong you are.

The best way to put this into practice is for students to be doing more self-marking of their own work and assessments. There will obviously have to be some training, guidance and modelling here but, once students get used to this process, it can be a very useful tool for learning, not just measurement. By talking through the answers, modelling what a good one looks like (WAGOLL) and deconstructing answers at a range of levels, you start to involve students in the evaluation of their work rather than just providing them with feedback that they may or may not choose to read. Reviewing and correcting their own work (especially if they are not just doing this to reach the next grade boundary but because they have an intrinsic motivation to do better) can play a significant part in their own learning. If done correctly, self-assessment can therefore become another learning tool, rather than just being seen as an assessment tool. The more students use it and become skilled at it, the more useful it will become in their learning.

**TEACHING TIP**

*One of the easiest ways to introduce this is to do more testing and less marking. By combining the research on retrieval practice (see page 3) and assessment (see page 52), along with the hypercorrection effect of feedback, you can not only increase your effective use of formative assessment but also reduce your workload at the same time.*

# FURTHER READING

If you want to continue your reading around feedback and how to make sure that the time you spend on it is in proportion to the impact it has on learning outcomes, here are some useful starting points.

▶ **Researchers:** Dylan Wiliam, Alfie Kohn, Craig Barton.

▶ **Publications:** Dylan Wiliam (2011), *Embedded Formative Assessment.* Bloomington, IN: Solution Tree Press.

Alfie Kohn (2011), 'The case against grades', *Counterpoints*, 451, 143–153.

Wiliam, D. (2016), 'Dylan Wiliam – author, researcher, trainer and assessment for learning expert', Interview for Mr Barton Maths Podcast, www.mrbartonmaths.com/blog/dylan-wiliam-author-researcher-trainer-and-assessment-for-learning-expert

Hendrick, C. and Macpherson, R. (2017), *What Does This Look Like in the Classroom?* Woodbridge: John Catt.

▶ **Keyword search:** Feedback; marking; marking and feedback; feedforward; hypercorrection effect; grading; constructive comments; whole-class feedback.

# PERSONAL REFLECTION

How has your use of feedback evolved over the course of
your teaching career?

Thinking about the time that you spend on student feedback, do you feel
that this is reflected in the impact it has on raising achievement?

Having now reflected on the research on feedback, how might you change
your approach to providing feedback, so that you can ensure it has the biggest
impact on raising achievement while also not creating excessive workload?

# CHAPTER 7

# LEARNING VERSUS PERFORMANCE

Can
you really see
learning, or do you only see
the performance of a child at any
given time? In this chapter we will
look at the difference between learning
and performance and how teachers can
construct assessment opportunities in
the most effective conditions
in order to make the most
accurate inferences about
real learning.

# TEACHER 1.0

**1.0**

If you strip teaching back to its most simplistic form, you teach a new concept to a group of students and then test them on that new knowledge to see how much of it they have understood and remembered. The score that a student gets on a test is widely seen as a good indicator of how much the student has learned. The greater the score, the more a student has learned, and the lower the score, the less they have learned. This crude method of testing has been around for centuries and used in scenarios not just in education, but in everything from learning your first ever list of spellings to how to drive your first car. However, the score that is generated by the test is not always a strong or accurate indicator of real *learning* but instead of your *performance* on that specific test on that specific day. The problem with this has been that too many people have not had the insight to question the merits of the score and have mistakenly taken it as proof of how much you have learned or not learned.

Think back to your driving test (especially if you did not pass first time around). Were you actually a significantly improved driver the second or third time around when you passed? Or did you just 'perform' better in that test and not make a silly mistake or mental error this time around? Think also about your favourite sports team. Do they always 'perform' at a consistent level? Or do they sometimes have significant and unexplained dips in performance against teams who are generally perceived to be below their level? If tests always demonstrated our accurate levels of learning, then 'performance' would not come into the equation – but we know from personal experience that it isn't always that straightforward.

For Teacher 1.0, the worrying thing is that, although we have shown that performance can be a factor in our own lives, we have tended to ignore this fact when it has come to testing in our own classrooms. Raw scores from tests have been inputted into spreadsheets and digital tracking systems and have been seen as an accurate picture of the learning and progress from your students. These scores have then been converted into colour-coded statements that relate to whether a student is on track or not, resulting in intervention strategies either being put in place, or a student being left to their own devices. However, based on how a student has actually 'performed' on that specific test, their score may have either been positively inflated or negatively reduced based on a whole host of factors that may have been either inside or outside of our control as the classroom teacher. Whether we like it or not, there are many ways in which we, as teachers, influence the performance of our students on a day-to-day basis. Once you combine this with the external influences that also have a significant bearing on how our students perform, you suddenly begin to see how the scores that we have been reporting and making inferences about may not be as accurate as you once thought.

# FACTORS THAT INFLUENCE PERFORMANCE

Here are some of the most common ways in which performance can be influenced. The list is split into external factors that are *out* of our control and factors *within* our control, and considers how each factor can positively or negatively contribute to the learning versus performance debate.

External factors out of our control:

▶ **Hunger:** Has the student had any breakfast this morning? Can they concentrate if they are hungry? Have they got the required amount of energy to perform at a high level throughout a 90-minute exam?

▶ **Illness:** If a student has a cold or a headache, will this have a negative impact on their ability to concentrate and focus on a demanding assessment?

▶ **Home life:** If there has been an argument in the house between a student's parents, or between the student and their parents, how will this affect their mood coming into the assessment? Will they be in the right frame of mind to give their very best or will the situation at home be on their mind?

▶ **Sleep:** We all know that we are not at our best if we have not had enough sleep, so will a student be able to perform if they have been up all night on their console or not been able to sleep through illness or a crying baby in the house?

▶ **No revision:** If a student has not bothered to do any revision, is this a true reflection of their best attempt at an assessment, especially if others in the class have taken the time to revise for the assessment?

▶ **Some revision:** A student may have decided to do some last-minute cramming before an assessment or exam and got lucky with the topic they have chosen to revise. If this topic has come up on the exam, then they might receive a significantly higher score than they would have received if any of the other topics had appeared.

Factors within our control:

▶ **Revision session:** If we plan to teach a 'revision session' the day before an assessment, we will always cover the topics that are going to appear on the test. This way, we are giving significant clues to the students about what is going to appear in the test.

▶ **Writing the test yourself:** If you combine the fact that you are delivering a revision session the day before the test with the fact that you have actually written the test yourself, then, whether you are conscious of this or not, you are always going to be directing your students' attention to the topics that they will be tested upon.

▶ **Classroom displays:** If you teach in a classroom with great learning displays up on the walls, and then you test your students in this same classroom, the chances are you might see students looking up to the walls for help with some of the answers.

▶ **Assessment complexity:** As we discussed in Chapter 5, page 54, the more complex the wording of your questions, the greater the chance of students not doing well for reasons that have nothing to do with their knowledge of the subject.

▶ **Spacing:** If you don't space out your assessments as we discussed in Chapter 2, page 13, and Chapter 5, page 48, there will be no time for forgetting and no level of desirable difficulty. Therefore, performance will be inflated due to familiarity and not learning.

▶ **Interleaving:** If you don't mix up the skills that students have to demonstrate on the assessment, it becomes far too easy because they already know what is coming next. As we mentioned in Chapter 3 on interleaving, page 25, students need to experience a level of desirable difficulty by identifying a problem and then comparing and contrasting between the solutions in order to solve it.

If Teacher 1.0 has been taking test results at face value and has never thought about how the performance of an individual student could have been positively or negatively influenced by one or more of these factors, then the very foundations on which we have built our assessment and intervention strategies have been pretty weak. Although we cannot change, eradicate or influence some of these factors, we still need to understand them so that we can limit their impact on how we assess real learning and not just the performance of a student on one particular day.

# WHAT DOES THE RESEARCH SAY?

Although some of the foundational studies in the research around learning versus performance are from the 1930s, 1940s and 1950s, the main pedagogical research on the difference between learning and performance and the implications this has on teaching, training and general instruction have only been written and more widely understood since the 1990s. There are also two major studies that are even more recent than that and it is these papers that we will explore in this chapter:

▶ Richard A. Schmidt and Timothy D. Lee. (2011), *Motor Control and Learning: A behavioural analysis* (5th edn.). Leeds: Human Kinetics.

▶ Nicholas C. Soderstrom and Robert A. Bjork (2015), 'Learning versus performance: An integrative review', *Perspectives on Psychological Science*, 10, (2), 176–199.

## RICHARD A. SCHMIDT AND TIMOTHY D. LEE

In their book *Motor Control and Learning: A behavioural analysis*, Schmidt and Lee provide a very useful distinction between performance during acquisition and long-term learning. Their work around acquisition, and retention and transfer, implies that learning should be distinguished from temporary performance enhancement, and that learning cannot be directly observed but instead must be inferred from changes in performance over a period of time. Schmidt and Lee make it very clear that, if we are looking to measure a permanent change in capability and not just in performance during practice, then this must be measured by tests that demonstrate retention after the completion of practice. An improved capability should not only be observable during practice but should be retained over time.

 **Learning should be distinguished from temporary performance enhancement.**

 **Learning cannot be directly observed, but instead must be inferred from changes in performance over a period of time.**

Their clear distinction between learning and performance also implies that spacing is imperative in how we plan the delivery of our curriculum. By making significant references to 'performance during practice', Schmidt and

Lee are describing a delivery model where content is blocked together and any testing or measuring of 'learning' is done within that time period. As we already know, there are a multitude of different reasons why performance might not reflect real learning during practice or blocked teaching. Schmidt and Lee's constant reference to the words 'retention and transfer' makes it abundantly clear that, if we really want to measure long-term learning, we must construct test conditions that do just that. We need to see whether our students can retain information and transfer it to unfamiliar situations long after we have stopped teaching or practising that skill or content. Giving students time to forget information, and testing them at a later date via intelligent spacing of content and assessments, is vital in this process.

Schmidt and Lee draw the conclusion that the general failure to distinguish between performance during practice, and retention and transfer, has resulted in a history of misconceptions and inaccurate inferences about learning and performance. However, with the more recent literature around this subject over the past 25 years, it is now well established that performance during practice is a poor predictor for retention and transfer. Just because performance might improve during practice or initial instruction does not mean that retention or transfer will happen at a later date. To enable more accurate inferences around long-term learning and not just short-term performance, it is necessary to test well after the practice or initial instruction has stopped.

**Performance during practice is a poor predictor for knowledge retention and transfer. To enable more accurate inferences around long-term learning and not just short-term performance, it is necessary to test well after the practice or initial instruction has stopped.**

## NICHOLAS C. SODERSTROM AND ROBERT A. BJORK

Soderstrom and Bjork's (2015) work was one of the first pieces of literature to integrate countless foundational studies in this area and bring about a coherent and comprehensive view on learning versus performance. They begin with a simple and clear statement that Teacher 1.0 should have been told years ago: 'The goal of instruction is to facilitate learning, which must be inferred at some point after instruction. Learning, however, must be distinguished from performance, which is what can be observed and measured during instruction or training'. It is therefore crucial to understand that true learning must be measured after a period of time when direct input from the teacher has stopped.

 **'Learning refers to relatively permanent changes in knowledge or behaviour. It is – or at least should be – the goal of education.' (Soderstrom and Bjork, 2015)**

In a more recent article 'Learning vs. performance: A distinction every educator should know', Soderstrom (2019) provides his own individual distinction between the two terms: 'Learning refers to relatively permanent changes in knowledge or behaviour. It is – or at least should be – the goal of education. Performance, on the other hand, refers to temporary fluctuations in knowledge or behaviour that can be measured or observed during (or shortly after) instruction.' Both of these statements, distinctions and definitions make the differences between learning and performance extremely clear and give us food for thought when reflecting on how Teacher 1.0 may have been trying to measure learning in the past.

 **'Performance refers to temporary fluctuations in knowledge or behaviour that can be measured or observed during (or shortly after) instruction.' (Soderstrom, 2019)**

Aside from their succinct definitions of learning and performance, Soderstrom and Bjork also offer us very interesting findings that demonstrate not only that short-term performance is a poor indicator of long-term learning, but also how learning and performance can actually be inversely related. In simple terms, when one is raised, the other may be lowered.

 **Learning and performance are usually found to be inversely related.**

As we have already mentioned in this chapter and previous chapters (and has been well documented by Schmidt and Lee), there is no doubt that short-term performance gains can fail to support long-term learning gains. This is especially true if the performance gains are achieved by using teaching strategies (such as blocking) that are designed to produce rapid progress. But what about the flip side? Soderstrom and Bjork questioned the notion that 'if increased performance can lead to decreased learning, can *decreased* performance lead to *increased* learning?' Through their integrated research of many foundational studies and their knowledge of human memory, the answer they found was yes. They comment that 'as counterintuitive as it sounds, long-term learning can be enhanced by intentionally impairing short-term performance. The conditions that induce the most errors during acquisition are often the very conditions that lead to the most learning'. In practice, this means that implementing desirable difficulties, through spacing and interleaving for example, might not improve performance initially, but will enhance long-term learning.

 **By making learning harder, through imposing a series of carefully thought-out desirable difficulties, you may hinder initial performance, but you will be supporting long-term learning.**

This takes us back to Bjork's previous work on 'desirable difficulties', which we referenced in Chapters 2, 3 and 4. Soderstrom and Bjork point out that, if introduced intelligently and effectively, desirable difficulties are the factors that lead to an inversely related relationship between learning and performance. 'They are desirable because they lead to better long-term retention and transfer of knowledge, and they are difficult because they pose challenges that slow the rate of current progress and induce more mistakes during instruction or training.' Soderstrom and Bjork also tell us not to worry about potentially hindering or restricting short-term performance by introducing these desirable difficulties. In fact, the clue is in the name – 'desirable'. They say that 'as a rule of thumb, if students aren't struggling a bit – that is, if their performance isn't somewhat hindered – they're probably not engaged with the material in ways that will lead to meaningful, long-term comprehension and understanding'. Bjork has a great takeaway message for all teachers on this subject: 'Be suspicious of the sense of ease and undeterred by the sense of difficulty.'

 **If you feel that students are too confident and learning feels easy, there's every chance that it hasn't been sufficiently desirably difficult to promote deep thinking and lead to long-term learning.**

# TEACHER 2.0

Now that we are familiar with the research and literature around learning and performance, let's take a look at some strategies that you can put into practice to ensure that you don't mistake short-term performance for long-term learning.

## IDEA 25: ADD SPACING TO YOUR ASSESSMENTS

*Don't just test your students while they're practising; give them time to forget.*

Linking together everything we have been learning about retrieval practice, spacing, assessment and learning versus performance, it is imperative that you leave some time between teaching a specific skill or piece of content and then testing it. As Schmidt and Lee point out, if we are looking to measure a permanent change in capability and not just performance during practice, then this must be measured by tests that demonstrate retention after the completion of practice. In this case, you need to give students time to almost forget what they have learned in order to recall it and demonstrate true learning and not just familiarity. Without this spacing delay, performance may be significantly increased due to a number of factors that we have already highlighted in this chapter.

The best way to do this is not to test the learning from a topic until you have taught another topic. For example, Teacher 1.0 would have taught Topic 1 and then tested on Topic 1 before moving on to Topic 2 and doing the same again. However, in this new strategy, you teach Topic 1 and then move on to Topic 2. At the end of Topic 2, you go back and test on Topic 1, thus giving students time to forget the information and then recall it again. This way, students will demonstrate far deeper knowledge of a subject if they can recall it, rather than just 'performing' quite well because it is still far too familiar.

**TEACHING TIP**

*Like we have discussed several times so far, it is extremely important to take time to sell the 'why' to your students regarding the spacing of your assessments and the desirable difficulties that you are placing upon them. Once you begin to talk to them about not wanting to place importance on 'performance', but instead on permanent changes in capability or knowledge retention over time, then it begins to shift the culture in the class away from last-minute cramming and towards a more mature approach to learning.*

# IDEA 26: RE-TEST AGAIN A WEEK LATER

*You might have performed quite well today, but let's see what you can remember in a week's time.*

Even if you space out your assessment from the initial content delivery, there may still be a significant element of the score that a student gets that is purely down to performance. This can be either a positive uplift or a negative reduction. As we have already talked about at the beginning of this chapter, some of the reasons for the positive or negative performance can be outside of our control, so we can never completely control the conditions in which we assess the learning of our students. However, one of the most common forms of inflated performance is last-minute cramming the night before an exam or assessment. Yes, the student might appear to have performed quite well the very next day, but the chances are the majority of information they crammed into their short-term memory will soon be lost.

One way to combat this and get a far more accurate picture of their long-term learning is to administer the same test or assessment one week later. By asking the exact same questions in a week's time, you will be able to see how much difference there is between the two scores. A significantly reduced score in the second test might demonstrate that not as much real learning has taken place as you may first have thought. A score close to, or even better than, that received on the first test may indicate a far more accurate picture of what students have actually learned and committed to long-term memory. Remember that there is always the chance that the second test has also been influenced by one or more of the factors discussed on page 79. Nevertheless, as long as you are aware of these possible factors, and you have gone back and tested for a second time, you are at least starting to minimise the impact of those factors on the inferences you are making about real learning.

**TEACHING TIP**

*If you always tell your students when the second test will be, then you might still get inflated performances due to students cramming the night before. The best way may be to administer the second test in a 'no notice' style. However, over time, students will be clever enough to switch on to when you do this. If you always do it in the next lesson, or exactly one week after the first test, they will begin to prepare for this happening. Try to mix up when you do the test, so that you get the most accurate information possible.*

# IDEA 27: STOP DELIVERING REVISION SESSIONS THE LESSON BEFORE AN ASSESSMENT

*Let me give you some clues about what I'm going to ask you on the assessment tomorrow.*

As we have already discussed in Chapter 5, page 48, many teachers still write their own end-of-unit tests and 'in-class' assessments. Although we have talked about the issues that may arise from this, it is compounded further when a teacher not only designs their own assessment but also delivers a revision session to their students the lesson before that assessment. The problem with this approach is that there isn't a teacher on the planet who would deliberately deliver a revision session on topics that were not about to come up in the test or assessment that they had just written. Therefore, although the teacher is doing this with the best intentions and to try to help students 'perform' as best as they can, they are significantly inflating the 'performance' of the students by giving them clues as to what will appear on the test.

If you really want to plan time for students to revise before a test and you can't be sure that they will be independent enough to do this on their own outside of the classroom, you may want to schedule some time for independent retrieval practice in your lesson. By using this method, you are not influencing performance by delivering a session related to the topics on the test and instead you are giving time over to the students to do their own self-quizzing or peer-quizzing, which you can supervise. This also means that you can check the revision skills and strategies that your students are using, stopping them from using bad habits such as re-reading old notes, which, as we have already discussed in Chapter 2, page 13, have very little impact on long-term learning.

**TEACHING TIP**

*Ask students to create their own flashcards to facilitate their self-quizzing retrieval practice or work with friends to quiz each other. By taking time to work with students on the best way to create flashcards and then, more importantly, the best way to use them, you are not only limiting your own influence on the students in preparation for an end-of-unit test, but also helping them to build great study habits. The most effective way to use flashcards is to write one question (only one) on one side of the card, followed by the answer on the reverse. Students can then get family members to ask them the questions or they can self-quiz by reading the question and only turning over for the answer once they have answered the question independently.*

# IDEA 28: USE MULTIPLE ASSESSMENTS TO MAKE INFERENCES ABOUT REAL LEARNING

*Just because they performed in a certain way on this assessment doesn't mean to say that it's the only measure I'm going to use to make a judgement on how much they have learned.*

We all have off-days and we can all think of times when we have over- or underperformed on various aspects in our own lives. The same can be said for our students. If we only ever use one assessment or test to measure the learning of a specific skill or topic, then we may be making significantly inaccurate judgements based on the 'performance' of an individual in a particular set of circumstances. If this judgement is then inputted into a spreadsheet and used for student tracking purposes, we may find that this isn't worth the paper it's written on by the time a student comes to take their final examinations. By using a multitude of assessments, including low-stakes quizzing and formative assessments, we can begin to use a wealth of information to look past individual performances and begin to focus more on real learning.

The best way to do this is not to use a single assessment to inform the score that you enter into a spreadsheet or student tracking software. Yes, the score from that specific assessment may give you a steer as to how much they have actually learned, but an experienced teacher should know far more about that student and how much they have learned based on a number of other pieces of information that they hold about that student. Once all of these pieces of information have been processed by the teacher (either mentally or physically in a mark book), only then does the teacher have sufficient evidence to make an informed and accurate inference about the learning that the specific student has gained. This process may take more time but you will undoubtedly be making more accurate judgements, along with being able to potentially spot where 'performance' has either significantly increased or decreased.

> **TEACHING TIP**
> *By analysing where student performance has significantly increased or decreased across a whole class, you may be able to use these trends to begin to understand how you may have influenced performance in some way. Did your revision session significantly increase performance? Did the complexity of your questions have a negative impact on how the students performed? Once you begin to look at your teaching in this way, you can start to reduce the amount of influence you have on performance only – allowing you to get a better sense of the actual learning taking place.*

# FURTHER READING

If you want to continue your reading into learning versus performance and the inferences you are making about long-term learning, here are some useful starting points.

▶ **Researchers:** Richard A. Schmidt, Timothy D. Lee, Nicholas C. Soderstrom, Robert A. Bjork, Daisy Christodoulou.

▶ **Publications:** Richard A. Schmidt and Timothy D. Lee. (2011), *Motor Control and Learning: A behavioural analysis* (5th edn.). Leeds: Human Kinetics.

Nicholas C. Soderstrom and Robert A. Bjork (2015), 'Learning versus performance: An integrative review', *Perspectives on Psychological Science*, 10, (2), 176–199.

Nicholas Soderstrom (2019), 'Learning vs. performance: A distinction every educator should know', https://medium.com/age-of-awareness/learning-vsperformance-a-distinction-every-educator-should-know-aa165a83a4f9

Daisy Christodoulou (2017), *Making Good Progress? The future of assessment for learning.* Oxford: Oxford University Press.

▶ **Keyword search:** Learning; long-term learning; performance; performance gains; retention; transfer; desirable difficulties; assessment; spacing; revision.

# PERSONAL REFLECTION

Reflecting on this chapter, how accurate do you think your inferences on student learning have been up to this point in your career? What do you think the biggest influences have been on student performance in your classroom? Consider factors for which you have been responsible and those that have been outside of your control.

Having now reflected on the research on learning versus performance, how might you change your approach to assessments, so you can ensure that you are making the most accurate inferences possible about long-term learning and not just performance?

# CHAPTER 8

# COGNITIVE LOAD

The
working memory
of our brain can only
cope with a certain amount of
information at any one time. In this
chapter we will look at what
cognitive load means for us as teachers
and how it impacts on learning.
There are then practical ideas for
how you can manage the cognitive
demands that you place
upon your students every
lesson.

# TEACHER 1.0

**1.0**

One thing that teachers have never been able to do is to look inside a child's brain. No matter how experienced or skilled we think we are as professionals, we have never been able to accurately identify when our delivery of content has been too much for an individual or a class of students. Unfortunately, there is no red warning light or LED indicator to inform us when we are reaching the cognitive load threshold and sending our students into a state of cognitive overload. Worse still, until the research of John Sweller in 1988, this had never been something that teachers had really thought about. And even now, over 30 years later, many teachers are still not familiar with the cognitive science that governs how much information a student can process at any given time. Without this understanding of cognitive science and the links to what we teach and how we teach it, there have probably been numerous students in every one of our lessons over the course of our career for whom, if you had looked inside their heads, you would have seen those red lights flashing.

Even though this lack of knowledge about cognitive science has been prevalent for many years, the dawn of the interactive whiteboard has served to make things even worse. Putting the creative possibilities of Microsoft PowerPoint in the hands of Teacher 1.0, along with the use of an interactive whiteboard and a projector to help display classroom resources, was supposed to aid classroom delivery and bring it out of the dark ages. However, in far too many cases, the infinite fonts, background colours, transitions and moving clipart have only increased the amount of information that our students have had to process, thus resulting in regular occurrences of cognitive overload. Even more worryingly, it is only recently that we have been starting to understand the negative implications that some of our new-fangled technology has been having on our students' cognitive load. In fact, the technology has never been the problem; it is the way that we have seen fit to use it, getting carried away with the sudden explosion of digital tools and our ability to do things that you could never have done with an overhead projector and acetate.

Although the research will demonstrate many other ways in which cognitive load can be managed by teachers, one of the quickest and easiest ways to do this is to think carefully about our use of digital technology and the presentation slides that we put together. Take a look at the following ways in which Teacher 1.0 has been putting their PowerPoint presentations together, in the hope that they will engage students to sit up and take notice, when in reality they have probably been sending them into cognitive overload:

▶ **Hard-to-read fonts:** The desire to make our presentations fancy has led us to picking some random and hard-to-read fonts from time to time. If your brain is struggling to read the font at first glance and you have to pay extra attention to focus just on reading what has been written, this takes extra brain power in your working memory and therefore reduces your capacity to use it elsewhere.

▶ **Colourful background themes:** You can spend all day choosing a colourful theme to make your presentation stand out. However, some of these backgrounds tend to be a distraction to the student, with their minds and eyes immediately looking at the lines, images and different effects that the theme has to offer, instead of focusing on what is important: the content. In some themes, text can also be difficult to distinguish and read, putting even more strain on that already overloaded working memory.

▶ **Animated images:** The dawn of digital technology and the internet has a lot to answer for, including flashing and moving images appearing all over PowerPoint slides in schools. Imagine you have to focus on something straight ahead, but there is something else constantly moving in the corner of your eye line. It would either take all your mental power of focus and resilience not to keep glancing at that distraction, or you would end up looking at it from time to time, losing your focus on what you had been told to concentrate on.

▶ **Too much text:** Just because you can fit hundreds of words on one PowerPoint slide doesn't mean you have to. As soon as you place words on a screen, people will naturally want to read them. If you want them to listen to what you are saying while the slide is on the screen, this starts to create a conflict of choice in the working memory: students are torn between reading and listening, and it becomes very difficult to do either effectively.

▶ **Reading slides to students:** By simply reading out the words on the slides to your students, you are sending their working memory into overload. The chances are that, if you have put text up, students will already have started reading it, so when you begin reading it to them, you are probably a little out of sync with the voice in their head that is reading it to them. Therefore, there are now two voices competing for their focus, thus making it significantly harder for them to concentrate on what they, or you, are reading.

▶ **Too busy:** If your slides have text, images, diagrams and moving parts all thrown together on one slide, it can be extremely difficult for students to pick out what is important and then focus on it. Many things will be competing for their attention and therefore using up far too much of their working memory, leaving them too little to process the difficult learning tasks that you want them to do. White space is good for cognitive load – think Google.

Cognitive load is not something that we can control completely and we will never be able to see inside our students' heads to know whether we have got it right, but there are (as we have just seen) some obvious ways to guard against situations that limit the amount of working memory that our students are left with to solve the challenging learning tasks that we give them.

# WHAT DOES THE RESEARCH SAY?

Research on cognitive science in education and its implications for classroom teachers is a relatively new kid on the block. John Sweller's work on cognitive load began in the late 1980s. In this research, Sweller (1988) described cognitive load as a point in time when multiple sources of information or interactive elements need to be processed simultaneously, leaving insufficient working memory to solve or complete the task at hand. However, over 30 years later, Sweller's work is still not widely understood or adopted by the masses. This is even more concerning given that, in 2017, Dylan Wiliam said that he had 'come to the conclusion that Sweller's Cognitive Load Theory is the single most important thing for teachers to know'.

 **According to Dylan Wiliam, cognitive load theory 'is the single most important thing for teachers to know'.**

The two pieces of research that I have included highlights from in this section summarise cognitive load theory and working memory extremely well, providing teachers with a great insight into its implications when it comes to lesson delivery.

▶ Fred Paas, Alexander Renkl and John Sweller (2003), 'Cognitive load theory and instructional design: Recent developments', *Educational Psychology*, 38, (1), 1–4.

▶ Susan Gathercole and Tracy Packiam Alloway (2007), *Understanding Working Memory, A Classroom Guide* (2nd edn.). London: Sage.

# FRED PAAS, ALEXANDER RENKL AND JOHN SWELLER

Building on Sweller's original work on cognitive load from 1988, Paas, Renkl and Sweller's 2003 paper highlights the significant interest that had developed in cognitive load theory from researchers across the globe by the early noughties. In this paper, they divide cognitive load into three distinct categories – intrinsic, extraneous and germane – demonstrating the different ways in which our working memory can be placed into overload if we are not careful.

## INTRINSIC COGNITIVE LOAD

Intrinsic cognitive load is where the material or the content is at a level that the learner finds too difficult to process or manage given their current level of knowledge, experience or proficiency. This means that the teacher's understanding of the prior knowledge of the students is absolutely vital in managing their cognitive load. Teachers need to present students with a certain degree of intrinsic cognitive load if they are to challenge them appropriately, but they must be careful not to overdo it. There are ways to reduce the intrinsic cognitive load of students, even when presenting them with new or challenging content. Teachers can break down complex ideas and topics into smaller sub-sections, for example, so students can master each foundational concept, rather than introducing them all at once. By not overwhelming novice learners with too many complex ideas at once, you can effectively manage the capacity of their working memory.

 **If the content is too difficult or unfamiliar to a student, it will occupy a significant amount of their working memory.**

## EXTRANEOUS COGNITIVE LOAD

Paas, Renkl and Sweller refer to this type of cognitive load as being associated with an unnecessary amount of working memory taken up by 'activities that are irrelevant to schema acquisition and automation'. In other words, where our brain has to spend more time and effort either looking for the information, trying to process it, or having to shut out various other distractions, it creates unnecessary strain on our already stretched working memory, meaning we have less capacity to use on the things we need it for most.

If our brain has to spend more time and effort looking for information, trying to process it, or having to shut out various other distractions, it creates unnecessary strain on our already stretched working memory.

Interestingly, the researchers also concluded that minimising extraneous cognitive load is more important when the level of intrinsic cognitive load is high because the two forms of cognitive load add together. However, when intrinsic cognitive load is low, levels of extraneous cognitive load are less important because total cognitive load will probably not exceed your working memory capacity. Teachers can reduce this type of cognitive load by paying careful attention to the way in which information is presented and not making the same mistakes that we have already discussed in the Teacher 1.0 section of this chapter (page 92).

 If the level of intrinsic cognitive load is low, you don't need to worry as much about the level of extraneous cognitive load, because the total cognitive load being experienced may not exceed working memory capacity.

## GERMANE COGNITIVE LOAD

Despite adding to overall cognitive load, germane load is a positive type of cognitive load as it is essential for storing new information in the long-term memory by connecting it to pre-existing schema (a cognitive framework and neurological map that helps us organise and interpret information and link knowledge together). This creates automation in the future. This type of cognitive load is a natural process that goes on inside the brain when we try to connect new information to prior learning and is therefore not directly influenced by the teacher. It is nevertheless vital that teachers understand the demands they are placing on their students via both intrinsic and extraneous cognitive load, so as to leave sufficient capacity for germane load to occur, without tipping the student over the threshold into cognitive overload.

 Not all cognitive load is negative. We require cognitive load to challenge students and store new information in the long-term memory by connecting it to pre-existing schema.

# SUSAN GATHERCOLE AND TRACY PACKIAM ALLOWAY

Using the research on cognitive load theory as a basis for further development and investigation, Gathercole and Alloway take a deeper look at working memory in their book, *Understanding Working Memory: A classroom guide*. As part of this further investigation into working memory in children, one of the most important points that Gathercole and Alloway make is that, unsurprisingly, the level of working memory will vary between individual people. This means that, even if you estimate the level of working memory required for a task and the level of cognitive load that it will occupy, it will still pose a different challenge for everyone. A particular activity may be well within the capacity of one person but exceed that of another.

 **Working memory levels are different for each student. An activity may be well within the capacity of one student but exceed that of another, so think carefully about the level of challenge when planning tasks.**

Gathercole and Alloway also state that, in terms of the development of children, 'working memory capacity also increases with age during childhood. Young children typically have very small capacities that increase gradually until the teenage years, when adult capacities are reached that are more than double that of 4-year-old children'. Although this may sound quite obvious, it is important to remember it when planning learning activities and designing lesson resources for children of different age groups.

 **Working memory capacity increases with age during childhood.**

Gathercole and Alloway's book not only outlines the importance of working memory for children and how it is crucial for learning, but also gives teachers specific advice on how to support children with a low working memory. Below are some key features of that advice:

▶ **Recognise working memory failures:** This can manifest itself in the following ways: incomplete recall, failing to follow instructions, place-keeping errors and task abandonment. If these types of activity failure are observed, it is recommended that the working memory demands of the task are considered and, if believed to be excessive, the activity should be repeated with reduced working memory loads. In order to spot the working memory failures, you need to monitor the students in your class by either looking for the warning signs or by speaking to them directly about the demands of the tasks you have designed and delivered.

▶ **Evaluate the working demands of learning activities:** Teachers need to think about the cognitive demands they are placing on students and whether they are overloading their working memory. By linking back to the three different types of cognitive load in the research paper by Paas, Renkl and Sweller, you can begin to try to measure whether the task will cross the threshold of cognitive overload. If, after evaluating the working demands of your learning activities, you feel that cognitive load will be compromised, you need to think carefully about how you can reduce this load. This can be achieved in many ways, including reducing the processing demands, simplifying the delivery and structure of the information, increasing the familiarity of the information and utilising memory aids for students.

# TEACHER 2.0

Now that we have got to grips with the research and foundation knowledge around cognitive load and working memory, let's take a look at some strategies that you can put into practice to ensure that you don't place your students into cognitive overload.

### IDEA 29: INCREASE STUDENTS' GENERAL KNOWLEDGE AROUND THE SUBJECT

*Knowing things helps you to know more things.*

One way to reduce the amount of cognitive load on a student, especially when your content is challenging and demanding, is to gradually increase their general subject knowledge. If students have lots of general knowledge about your subject and it is already automated in their long-term memory, then this releases a significant proportion of their working memory to process the challenging and demanding tasks that you are wanting them to do in the lesson. If, however, they are having to try to remember some of the most basic facts and it is taking quite a lot of brain power from their working memory to do this, then there is not going to be sufficient capacity left to deal with the more complex tasks that make up the intrinsic cognitive load.

Knowing lots of facts also helps you to know lots of other things and connect seemingly random information together to form a schema of information. Without a deep base knowledge in the subject, new knowledge that students need to learn can seem like a tiny piece of a jigsaw – it's impossible to see where it fits into the bigger picture. This makes it extremely difficult to recall it at a later date because you are trying to remember thousands of unconnected facts. However, once you connect a fact to an existing fact or piece of knowledge that is already consigned to your long-term memory, it becomes far easier to remember because you can immediately see its place and relevance to the bigger picture.

**TEACHING TIP**

*Help students to gain this general subject knowledge by encouraging them to read around the subject. A great way to do this is to use homework tasks to provide topical articles to read, so that students can see how different facts are important when it comes to bigger-picture issues or ideas. By letting students know that the more they read around their subject, the greater their knowledge and understanding will be, the more quickly they might fall into the habit of extra reading and grasp its importance in their learning journey.*

## IDEA 30: REMOVE DISTRACTIONS

### *Let's get students to focus on the main thing.*

In the Teacher 1.0 section of this chapter, we discussed the several multimedia mistakes that teachers have been making since the dawn of the interactive whiteboard. It is vital that Teacher 2.0 is aware of the cognitive distractions that digital technology can bring if not used correctly, and the impact this can have on the cognitive load we place on our students. While, at one stage, teaching was all about how flashy you could make your presentation slides, now more and more teachers are understanding cognitive science and sticking with simple and easy-to-read slides that are uncluttered. Think about choice of font, font size, theme colours, image and text placement, and so on. If it doesn't add any value to your lesson and the learning of the students, leave it off the slides.

Another thing that can compete for the students' attention is the classroom wall that your interactive whiteboard is situated on. When was the last time that you sat at the back of your classroom and looked at your interactive whiteboard? How busy is your classroom wall around the edges of the whiteboard? Are there lots of random posters and images that are competing for your students' attention or is the whiteboard the main focus on that wall? That is not to say that you should suddenly strip your classroom walls of all posters, but it is interesting to take some time to reflect on the experience of the student when they are looking at your whiteboard.

## IDEA 31: AVOID SPLIT ATTENTION AND MULTITASKING

***We want our students to give us 100 per cent of their attention.***

As a direct addition to the previous idea, if we get students to split their attention between two items (even if they are intrinsically linked), then this adds considerable amounts of extraneous load to our students. This usually happens when we use a graph, chart or image to highlight a point and then have the key information about the graphic aligned away from, or separate to, the graphic. Students then have to constantly refer from one place to the next on the whiteboard, trying to put the information together to make sense of it. This can be easily avoided by including any key information as part of the graphic (for example, labelling the chart with titles and totals), rather than having a separate table showing the information that the student has to find and constantly cross-reference between.

Although as human beings we often talk about our ability to multitask, this can be one of the most significant barriers to learning. Quite simply, if students are having to multitask, then they are giving less than 100 per cent effort, concentration and focus to each task they are undertaking. As we already know, there is only a certain amount of working memory that our students can work with, so, if we divide that in half because we are asking them to perform multiple tasks or process information from different sources at the same time, then there is no possible way that they can be giving each one their undivided attention. Multitasking may be great for productivity when you need to get things done, but it is an undesirable difficulty when it comes to learning.

## IDEA 32: FLIPPED LEARNING

*Give students time to process new information before asking them to do something with it.*

If you are not already familiar with the concept of flipped learning, it is a method of lesson delivery where you re-order the way in which you teach and deliver new content. Instead of teaching new material in class and then sending students home to do something with the knowledge that they have just acquired, flipped learning introduces the new content as pre-learning for homework and then students come into the class to do something with that new knowledge. The great advantage of this concept when it comes to reducing cognitive load is that students will already have had time (in their own time, and as much of it as they need) to process this information, digest it and make sense of it before they enter the classroom and are asked to do something with it.

By utilising this approach, we ensure students are not placed into cognitive overload when they are faced with situations of intrinsic cognitive load because they will already have had time to consider this information and break it down into smaller chunks if necessary, or go over it multiple times until it is understood. By doing this in their own time, away from the pressures of the classroom environment and their peers, this enables students to feel far more comfortable when approaching challenging situations, knowing that they can take their time to grasp the finer details. Once all students have a good foundational knowledge of the new content (or even if they are just familiar with it because they have already seen it), it reduces cognitive load by releasing more of the working memory to deal with the task in hand.

> **TEACHING TIP**
>
> *A great way to provide pre-lesson learning is to record a short video (or narrate over an existing PowerPoint presentation), talking about the main areas of knowledge that the students need to know in order to be successful in the lesson. Students can then take notes and bring these notes into the lesson as a study aid. By keeping the videos under ten minutes in length, they are bite-sized and easy for students to watch on their phone or via a computer.*

# FURTHER READING

If you want to continue your reading into cognitive load and the way in which you can control it in the classroom, here are some useful starting points.

▶ **Researchers:** Fred Paas, Alexander Renkl, John Sweller, Susan Gathercole, Tracy Packiam Alloway, Dominic Shibli, Rachel West.

▶ **Publications:** Fred Paas, Alexander Renkl and John Sweller (2003), 'Cognitive load theory and instructional design: Recent developments', *Educational Psychologist*, 38, (1), 1–4.

Susan Gathercole and Tracy Packiam Alloway (2007), *Understanding Working Memory, A Classroom Guide* (2nd edn.). London: Sage.

John Sweller (1988), 'Cognitive load during problem solving: Effects on learning', *Cognitive Science*, 12, (2), 257–285.

Dominic Shibli and Rachel West (2018), 'Cognitive load theory and its application in the classroom', *Impact*, (2).

▶ **Keyword search:** Cognitive load; cognitive overload; working memory; intrinsic load; extraneous load; germane load.

# PERSONAL REFLECTION

Reflecting on this chapter, do you think that you have been putting your students into unnecessary situations of cognitive overload from time to time? If so, what have been the factors that have contributed to this?

Have there been times in your own professional learning when you felt that the levels of cognitive load placed upon you crossed over into cognitive overload? Why was this?

Now that you understand the research on cognitive load, are there any changes that you will make either to your lesson delivery or to your classroom environment to reduce instances of cognitive overload in the future?

# CHAPTER 9

# DUAL CODING

People learn more effectively when they are presented with text alongside graphics or images, rather than just text on its own. In this chapter we will look at how we can use the theory of dual coding to increase the effectiveness of how we deliver new information, while avoiding gimmicks and distractions that may cause cognitive overload in students.

# TEACHER 1.0

**1.0**

Before interactive whiteboards and projectors became a regular feature in every classroom, there was a time when teachers used to have to present their information in a very different way. A piece of chalk and a blackboard used to be a teacher's best friends when it came to presenting information to their students, but it didn't give them time to design and prepare the information beforehand. The majority of teachers simply wrote up information that came to mind during instruction and delivery. This also meant that, if you weren't particularly great at drawing, information was strictly limited to text only.

Next came overhead projectors, sheets of acetate and a new age of presenting information. Acetates enabled teachers to prepare their information at home or away from the classroom, and even include different colours to make certain words stand out from others. However, yet again, unless you were a fairly skilled artist, acetates tended to just include bullet-pointed lists of text, highlighting the key points of the lesson.

Then came projectors and interactive whiteboards, meaning that it did not matter if you were a skilled artist or not; you could now use images and text to engage your students in your subject matter and bring life to your dated style of instruction and delivery. However, in lots of cases, this evolution hasn't really worked out as we once thought it would. In fact, many teachers fall into one of the two following Teacher 1.0 categories:

▶ **I've got it all going on:** As we mentioned in the previous chapter on cognitive load, these teachers have gone all out on everything that PowerPoint can handle. Multiple colours for backgrounds and fonts are being used; pictures are randomly scattered everywhere, together with an over-reliance on clipart and animated icons. If PowerPoint can do it, these teachers are using it. The problem is that, although the intention has been to jazz up their old and boring ways, these teachers have gone too far the other way and the vast array of colours, images and moving graphics have only served to throw their students into a state of cognitive overload.

▶ **Death by PowerPoint:** For this group of teachers, their ways have not changed over the years. Yes, their lesson resources have now become digital, but you probably still wouldn't notice any difference in the layout and content of their slides from the acetates that they used to carry around in plastic wallets. Text-heavy presentations are still king in this world, but only serve to turn off students and disengage them the minute they look at the bottom left of the PowerPoint and see there are 30 slides coming at them in the next 60 mins. Every now and again, an image might pop up, but, in the main, it is there to fill space and not to add any value to the delivery of the topic.

This hasn't necessarily been Teacher 1.0's fault; in most cases, it is simply down to the fact that the research on dual coding and the importance of accompanying text with relevant images has never really been fed down to classroom teachers in a scientific and pedagogical way. Teachers have used images, icons and clipart to try to make their lesson resources and PowerPoint slides more appealing and engaging to students, or simply to fill the white space around their bullet-pointed lists. A lack of education about why and how people learn more effectively when they are presented with text and graphics or images together, rather than just text on its own, has meant that over the past 20 years, teachers have missed countless opportunities to make learning stick more effectively. It is not that Teacher 1.0 hasn't had the tools at his or her fingertips, but it has been the lack of understanding among the whole profession that has led to these two groups of delivery styles still dominating our students' learning experiences in the classroom.

# WHAT DOES THE RESEARCH SAY?

As with cognitive load theory, which we discussed in Chapter 8, research on dual coding is a relative newcomer to the classroom compared with some of the other topics of the science of learning that we have explored in this book. Although Allan Paivio began his research on dual coding in 1971, his best-regarded work in this area came in 1986 and was then followed up with several studies in the years afterwards. However, until Oliver Caviglioli picked up this theory in 2019 and presented it in a dual-coded format, it had rarely been understood or even discussed by teachers and teacher training schools. However, with Caviglioli's work now seeming to hit the mainstream classroom, finally we are starting to see some of this research changing the habits of teachers in the way they present their information.

▶ Allan Paivio (1986), *Mental Representations: A dual coding approach.* Oxford: Oxford University Press.

▶ Oliver Caviglioli (2019), *Dual Coding with Teachers.* Woodbridge: John Catt.

# ALLAN PAIVIO

At the heart of Paivio's theory of dual coding is the realisation that information is processed by our working memory in two forms – verbal information and visual information. Verbal information is the information that we hear. For students in our classrooms, this means anything that teachers tell students and anything that is read to them, even if it is text on the whiteboard. Visual information is any non-verbal information that is presented to us. When we think of the experiences of the students in our classrooms, this means any images, videos or icons that are part of the instruction and lesson delivery method. As we have seen in the Teacher 1.0 section of this chapter, teachers have been using some or a combination of these, but with little or no strategic thinking into how they can complement each other in the learning process.

 **Information is processed by our working memory in two forms – verbal information and visual information. It's important to use both of these presentation methods in a strategic way to promote learning.**

Paivio points out that, although we use these two channels to process information, they are independent of each other. That means we can use just the verbal channel or just the visual channel to understand new information. However, the key feature of Paivio's research is that, when you combine these two channels and they work in tandem with each other, they encode information far more effectively in our long-term memory. This is where the term 'dual coding' comes from; it means encoding information in two separate ways but at the same time. Paivio states that, when this happens, a double memory trace is created in our long-term memory, meaning that it is significantly easier to retrieve this information back into our working memory at a later date.

 **The verbal and visual information channels work independently of each other. However, when you combine these two channels and they work in tandem with each other, they encode information far more effectively in our long-term memory.**

Although the main feature of his work on dual coding is increased retrieval strength due to the double memory trace that is created in our long-term memory, Paivio also started to see that verbal and visual connections enable us to understand new information far more easily and thus reduce our cognitive load. Since Paivio's foundation work on dual coding, this theory has been researched further in more recent times and the theory of the 'visual argument' has now been developed to describe how information in both mediums helps us to understand it more effectively. For areas of study where the demands of the subject content are high, it is important to think about how a 'visual argument' can be used to reduce the intrinsic load and enable students to process the information effectively and encode it in their long-term memory.

**When both information channels are used, a double memory trace is created in our long-term memory. This helps to manage and reduce cognitive load during the learning process and makes it significantly easier to retrieve this information at a later date.**

# OLIVER CAVIGLIOLI

Building on the initial theory of dual coding from Allan Paivio, Caviglioli has taken this research and presented it in a way that has made it accessible and engaging to teachers by modelling the dual coding method to communicate the research findings effectively. At the outset, Caviglioli is very keen to stress two things about dual coding that often get lost in translation when people don't have a deep enough understanding of the research and make assumptions based on the headlines:

▶ The visual side of dual coding has nothing to do with learning styles or people being visual learners. As we now know, the theory of 'learning styles' has been completely discredited in recent times.

▶ Dual coding is far more than just putting words and images together to promote better recall at some point in the future. Yes, dual coding helps, but there are so many more benefits too.

**Dual coding has nothing to do with learning styles or people being visual learners.**

In his book, Caviglioli stresses the importance and power of visual representations to accompany words, whether these are images or simple icons (the latter are becoming far more popular and sophisticated). Based on experience, theories and evidence, Caviglioli proposes six reasons why including visuals carefully and strategically in your teaching increases the effectiveness of your classroom delivery:

▶ **They focus your attention:** When used effectively (and not overused as we have seen in Teacher 1.0), visuals can draw your attention to the important elements of your display, avoiding distractions or confusion. However, linking to cognitive load theory, if the visual is too far away from the text, this can lead to 'split attention', so careful and intelligent placement of the graphic or icon is essential.

▶ **They activate prior knowledge:** An effective visual display or overview of a process can help to trigger prior knowledge. The merging and connecting of prior knowledge also support the learning of new information in the future.

▶ **They help manage cognitive load:** If graphic design is used effectively (with simple icons, colour to highlight key information and so on), this can lead to a far more efficient use of our working memory, where our attention is not diverted by irrelevant visuals that are competing for our attention. Instead our focus and attention are directed to where we need it most.

▶ **They help develop schema:** When an overview of a process or a timeline of events is supported by a visual or graphic representation, this enables us to view all of the relevant information in one go and encode it to our long-term memory more efficiently by developing a clear schema.

▶ **They help to transfer information back into the working memory:** The simpler and more organised the visual is, the easier it is to retain the information and, more importantly, transfer it back into the working memory when required. If designed well, it allows the student to focus on key points of the process, which in turn will activate deep understanding of each area.

▶ **They help to engage and motivate:** By adding carefully placed visuals in your presentation of information, you help to break up a 'wall of words', injecting some life into a potentially already dry subject matter. This not only helps with engagement and recall, but also lets students develop meaning from the graphics if 'intrinsic load' is high.

> **If used intelligently and strategically, dual coding can significantly increase the effectiveness of your classroom delivery.**

# TEACHER 2.0

Now we have taken a look at the research behind dual coding and what it means for us in the classroom, let's consider some ways in which you can capitalise on this research to enable your students to learn more effectively.

## IDEA 33: USE GRAPHICS AND TEXT TOGETHER

***Spice up your slides with carefully chosen and strategically placed graphics.***

Working on the most basic principle of dual coding, if you are presenting new information to your students, try to present the text alongside an image or graphic that adds some value or clarity to your information. However, the image must be carefully selected so that it does not significantly divert attention away from the information or cause confusion. Although the image may foster engagement, it is not there for entertainment purposes. A graphic or image that is flashing, moving or clearly not intelligently connected or linked with the information will only add to the students' cognitive load and fail to utilise the benefits of dual coding.

Careful consideration must also be given to the placement and size of the image or graphic that you use. A graphic that is too far away from the information to which you are wanting it to add value will result in the 'split attention' effect that we discussed in Chapter 8, page 100, meaning that the student has to expend valuable working memory in constantly cross-referencing the two sources of information. A graphic that is far too big in proportion to the information will lead to the student focusing all of their attention on the graphic and not enough on the important text or information. This is also the same if the image is too small. Unless the proportions of text and image are carefully considered, one will receive far more attention than the other.

## IDEA 34: ADD IMAGES TO FLASHCARDS

### Add an image to create an extra memory trace.

When students are creating their own revision flashcards as part of their independent study aids leading up to their exams, get them to add images alongside their answers on the back of their cards. Lots of students are now starting to use the research behind retrieval practice as part of their revision and independent study by creating flashcards to test themselves on key subject content. However, in the main, this is by writing a question on the front of the card followed by the answer on the back of the card. As we have learned though, this is only utilising one information channel in which to encode the information in the long-term memory.

By adding an image, photograph or graphic to accompany the answer on the back of the card, this will begin to add an extra memory trace of the specific information, meaning it will be far easier to retrieve this information at a later date. As long as the visual is clearly related to the answer or information, it does not matter in which format it is presented. However, as we have already learned, the simpler the image, the better it is. Depending on the information to be learned, a drawing, graph, table, chart, process overview or photograph could all be used effectively to help encode the information in the long-term memory.

# IDEA 35: INFOGRAPHICS

### Get the whole process on one page.

In some subjects, specific topics can have lots of interrelated information and data that need to be learned by the students. It can often be a complex job for both the students and the teacher to condense it into a source that gives an overview of all the key points. Infographics make this possible by presenting a significant amount of complex information quickly and clearly on one page or in one image. This is usually in the form of graphics and text connected together to make a larger image. Even though there is information contained in the infographic from multiple sources, the fact it is eye-catching and condensed into one medium allows it to be easily digestible.

In order to make your infographic effective, it needs to include some (if not all) of the following elements: colour, icons, graphics, text, data, facts, statistics, references and timeframes. However, as we have previously mentioned, don't get fooled into thinking that you can just throw lots of random information and images together and create an effective infographic for learning. One of the most important things to think about when planning and designing an infographic is to cut down all of the unnecessary information and focus on including only the essential information. Once you have done this, you then need to think about placement and alignment of your images and text so that connecting pieces of information are placed together to manage cognitive load.

**TEACHING TIP**

*Although you may find creating these infographics quite enjoyable (particularly if you are creative or have a flair for art and design), you do not have to be a creative genius to design them for your students. Luckily there are a whole host of websites and online services that can help you create stunning infographics for free. As long as you have planned the information that you want to present, have cut it down to the essentials and have the text ready to upload, these websites will do the rest. Just search 'create free infographic' to get started.*

# IDEA 36: PUT DATA IN TABLES

*Include connecting information in the same place.*

In many subjects, numerical data is presented to students and they are expected to understand it and then remember it. This can be extremely difficult if the data is embedded within sentences or long paragraphs, especially if it has not been highlighted with different colours or a graphic or icon. However, using the theory that visual information opens up a new channel to help encode information in the long-term memory, creating a table develops a visual representation of the data you are presenting, thus meaning that it is far more likely to be recalled at a later date, as opposed to a random numerical fact that is part of a heavily worded slide of information.

Connecting this information together in one place also has two further benefits. Firstly, it lets the students compare and contrast the data against other figures, thus making sense of it and its relative significance. Secondly, it creates a mental picture of the data, so that, rather than having to remember and recall ten separate numerical facts, the student can recall the image of the table that they have in their head, and remember far more effectively the data in the table based on the position it occupies and the relationship it has with the other data or information. In simple terms, you are asking students to remember and recall one thing, rather than a series of separate and unconnected numerical values.

**TEACHING TIP** *If you are using both tables and graphs to help visualise a piece of information, make sure that the table of data is positioned either next to the graph or as part of the graph. By separating the data table from the graph, all you are doing is adding to the 'split attention' effect and placing greater levels of cognitive load upon your students. In software like Microsoft Excel, Word and PowerPoint, tables can be easily created and these data tables can also be included as part of graphs.*

# FURTHER READING

If you want to continue your reading into dual coding and how you can use it to increase the effectiveness of your lesson delivery, here are some useful starting points:

▶ **Researchers:** Allan Paivio, Oliver Caviglioli, Ruth Colvin Clark, Chopeta Lyons.

▶ **Publications:** Allan Paivio (1986), *Mental Representations: A dual coding approach.* Oxford: Oxford University Press.

Oliver Caviglioli (2019), *Dual Coding with Teachers.* Woodbridge: John Catt.

Oliver Caviglioli (2018), 'Six ways visuals help learning', *Impact,* (2).

Ruth Colvin Clark and Chopeta Lyons (2010), *Graphics for Learning: Proven guidelines for planning, designing, and evaluating visuals in training materials* (2nd edn.). San Francisco, CA: Wiley.

▶ **Keyword search:** Dual coding; memory trace; channels of information; encoding; visual argument; visual representations; graphics; icons; infographics; flashcards.

# PERSONAL REFLECTION

Reflecting on this chapter, how well do you feel you have been using both visual and verbal information to create a double memory trace when delivering new information for students to learn?

Thinking about your own experiences of professional learning, how do you like to see information presented when you are trying to understand it for the first time?

Now that you understand the research on dual coding, are there any changes you will make to how you design your lesson resources or teaching slides to help encode information more efficiently in your students' long-term memory?

# CHAPTER 10

# METACOGNITION

Metacognition is
our ability to analyse
how we think and learn, and
to use this information to choose
an appropriate and effective strategy
for the task at hand. In this chapter
we will look at how we can use the
research behind metacognition in our
classrooms to help the students
we teach to become better
learners.

# TEACHER 1.0

For as long as I can remember, Teacher 1.0 has been caught up in a vicious educational cycle. At a macro level, with so much content to get through in our respective courses, there is undoubtedly a huge focus on content, content and more content. New learning seems to be happening right up until examination season with little time for anything else. Then there's exam preparation and the continuous links to how to be successful on terminal examinations and the specific skills you need to learn to be able to construct a high-scoring answer. Once we break that down into a micro level for each topic or unit, we can see that the same cycle exists and repeats itself for every topic until the terminal exams take place. The problem this has given us is that there has been a perceived lack of time for students to do anything other than follow this cycle. Teachers and students have been pressured into this cycle by the increased culture of accountability under new education reforms over the past 20 years, without the necessary time or breathing space to stop and reflect on the success or failures of the strategies and techniques that they have been using.

It's quite a strange phenomenon when you think about it, because in most of our daily lives we think metacognitively all of the time and see it as an integral part of our intelligent (yet subconscious) thinking. Alex Quigley makes this point extremely succinctly in the September 2018 edition of the 'Trialled and Tested' podcast from Evidence Based Education and the Education Endowment Foundation (Evidence Based Education, 2018). In this interview, Quigley likens metacognitive thinking to the thinking we all do before or after we take a journey in our car. He breaks down the thinking into the following steps:

Planning our journey:

▶ How far away are we going?

▶ How long should the journey take?

▶ What time of day is it? Will the time of day influence how long it takes?

▶ How many different routes are there to select from?

▶ Was the route that I took the last time I drove there an effective and efficient route?

▶ Given all of the information I have, which route will I choose to take today?

Evaluating the journey:

▶ How long did the journey actually take?

▶ Was it longer or shorter than expected? Why was this?

▶ Would you take this route again at that time of the day?

▶ What made the route that you picked successful or unsuccessful?

Every time that we get in and out of our car, we are probably thinking metacognitively about our strategic decision-making, without even being conscious of it. It has become a habitual and autonomous act that enables us to select the best and most appropriate strategy for the task in hand. Can you just imagine how much time we would waste on the road if we never thought like this and just got behind the wheel and began driving without any thought or strategy? But this is exactly what the students in Teacher 1.0's class keep doing. They are given a task and immediately set off trying to solve it, with little or no strategic thought into which strategies they are going to select to help them and, more importantly, what happened the last time they were faced with a similar task or problem.

There are two reasons why this might be the case in Teacher 1.0's classroom:

▶ When done effectively, metacognition is almost a subconscious process. What Teacher 1.0 needs to do is to bring the subconscious back into the conscious mind so that these processes can be highlighted, demonstrated and explicitly taught. By narrating the thought processes that we go through, we can make the implicit explicit.

▶ Even though the *Sutton Trust-EEF Teaching and Learning Toolkit* (Education Endowment Foundation, 2012) has highlighted metacognition as the second-highest-ranking strategy available to teachers (giving a +7 months score), far too many teachers still don't fully understand what it means. In my experience when speaking to lots of teachers and leaders from schools all over the country, they tend to talk about metacognition like it is the same as spacing, interleaving or retrieval practice – something to do with improving memory.

Until we can break both of these two elements down by making the research and strategies more accessible to all, our students will still be diving straight into problems, hoping they get lucky with the first strategy they pick and it will lead them to instant success.

# WHAT DOES THE RESEARCH SAY?

Although the term 'metacognition' was first introduced by John Flavell in 1979, many research papers have been written on this topic since that time, but have seldom made it into the classrooms of our schools for many of the reasons I have talked about in the first chapter of this book. There are, however, two great sources of knowledge and research on metacognition that simplify a potential cognitive minefield for teachers so that they can quickly understand this strategy, digest the key information and act upon it.

▶ David Perkins (1992), *Smart Schools: Better thinking and learning for every child.* New York, NY: Simon and Schuster.

▶ Alex Quigley, Daniel Muijs, Eleanor Stringer (2018), 'Metacognition and self-regulated learning: Guidance report'. London: Education Endowment Foundation.

## DAVID PERKINS

Building on the research that had already taken place to develop the term 'metacognition' and to describe what it is and how useful it is to learners, in 1992, David Perkins outlined and defined four different levels of metacognitive learners whom teachers would probably find in every class they taught. The aim was to help teachers to understand what metacognition looks like in a student, how they could identify it and, more importantly, how they could work on moving students up through the levels. Perkins' four levels are as follows:

▶ **Tacit learners:** Tacit learners are unaware of their metacognitive knowledge. They do not think about any particular strategies for learning and merely accept that they know something or not.

▶ **Aware learners:** Aware learners know about some of the kinds of thinking that they do, such as generating ideas, finding evidence and so on. However, thinking is not necessarily deliberate or planned.

▶ **Strategic learners:** Strategic learners organise their thinking by using problem-solving, grouping and classifying, evidence-seeking and decision-making. They know and apply the strategies that help them learn.

▶ **Reflective learners:** Reflective learners are not only strategic about their thinking but they also reflect upon their learning while it is happening, considering the success or failure of the strategies they are using and then revising them as appropriate.

Perkins also points out something that has been lost in the transfer of academic research to the classroom in many schools: that metacognition is not just as simple as a set of generic thinking skills that can be taught in a cross-curricular way. Many schools have tried this and implemented lessons on metacognition in PSHE or tutor time but, as Perkins points out, 'the metacurriculum is much more than thinking skills'. He goes on to say that 'whereas thinking skills usually are seen as cross-disciplinary, the metacurriculum emphatically includes discipline-specific skills'. It is therefore vitally important to remember that any effective use of teaching metacognitive strategies must be subject-specific and be taught and developed with students by their subject teacher. Only then will students be able to connect the dots and use these new, reflective and evaluative strategies to be effective learners in that specific subject domain.

 **Metacognition is not a simple set of generic thinking skills that can be taught in a cross-curricular way. A metacurriculum includes subject-specific skills.**

In a later paper (titled 'Making thinking visible'), Perkins and his co-author Ron Ritchhart stress how important it is for teachers to make thinking visible. In the paper, Ritchhart and Perkins (2008) ask teachers to 'consider how often what we learn reflects what others are doing around us […] we watch, we imitate, we adapt what we see to our own styles and interests'. In simple terms, humans often learn by imitating others and then adapting what we have learned so it works for us. However, 'imagine learning to dance when the dancers around you are all invisible', or 'imagine learning a sport when the players who already know the game can't be seen'. Ritchhart and Perkins state that, for the most part, this is what happens in our classrooms every day when we ask our students to learn how to think or get better at it. Most thinking in classrooms is invisible, so it's really difficult for students to copy, and therefore learn, good thinking skills. If we want our students to get better at thinking, they need to see it being modelled in order for them to replicate or imitate it. As a teacher, it is therefore not just enough to tell students what to do, or how to get better at it; you need to physically model your thinking around it, letting them in on your thought processes.

**Most thinking is invisible, so we need to make the implicit explicit and support students in developing their metacognitive skills.**

# ALEX QUIGLEY, DANIEL MUIJS AND ELEANOR STRINGER

The one thing that really stands out in the evidence summaries and guidance reports that the Education Endowment Foundation (EEF) produce is that they have already taken all of the relevant research from one specific area into account and made it easily accessible for teachers and school leaders in a number of digestible and concise formats. These include a ranked table of teaching and learning strategies and interventions (in which metacognition comes second, only behind feedback), a fully referenced guidance report to help apply the research in the classroom, and a summary poster containing the main recommendations that all schools should take if they want to implement and utilise the power of metacognitive thinking with their students.

The seven recommendations from the guidance report on metacognition by Alex Quigley, Daniel Muijs and Eleanor Stringer are as follows:

▶ **Teachers should acquire the professional understanding and skills to develop their students' metacognitive knowledge:** This begins with what we discussed in the Teacher 1.0 section of this chapter: having a clear understanding of what metacognition is and how you can use it to develop students' metacognitive knowledge of how they learn. However, as this can be quite an independent skill, teachers must support students through this process as they begin to plan, monitor and evaluate their own learning.

▶ **You should explicitly teach students metacognitive strategies, including how to plan, monitor and evaluate their learning:** As Perkins found out over 25 years earlier, for metacognitive strategies to be taught and demonstrated effectively, they need to be applied in relation to specific content and tasks. This means that, although some introduction to metacognition can be delivered generically, it has the most impact when demonstrated and taught by subject teachers, who can encourage students to use those strategies to solve specific problems.

▶ **It's important to model your own thinking to help students develop their metacognitive and cognitive skills:** Modelling by a skilled and experienced teacher has been seen as one of the most effective practices for improving learning. However, for too long, this approach has just been used to model the practical outcome of a task. Revealing the thought processes of an expert learner as they tackle a challenging task significantly helps to develop students' metacognitive skills.

 **Teachers need to regularly model their own thinking skills to their students.**

▶ **Set an appropriate level of challenge to develop students' self-regulation and metacognition:** As with most things, the level of challenge you give your students is crucial to the success of the task. Students need to be supported in developing and using metacognitive strategies in the first instance, but then gradually move towards more independent implementation of metacognitive thinking as experience, knowledge and age increases.

▶ **Promote and develop metacognitive talk in the classroom:** As well as explicit teacher modelling, classroom dialogue between both teacher and student, and student and student, can be used to develop metacognitive skills. This can help build good study habits around the use of metacognitive thinking and avoids metacognition being seen as a bolt-on that is only used by the teacher from time to time.

 **Metacognition should not be seen as a bolt-on. To develop metacognitive habits, metacognitive talk should be regularly promoted in the classroom.**

▶ **Explicitly teach students how to organise and effectively manage their learning independently:** As students move towards a more independent implementation of metacognitive thinking, they will need support and feedback from the teacher on how successfully they are implementing these strategies. You can only withdraw the support once you are confident that they are proficient in using these strategies and that the strategies they are selecting are successful for them.

▶ **Schools should support teachers to develop knowledge of these approaches and expect them to be applied appropriately:** Linked to the first of the recommendations, if teachers haven't got a deep professional understanding of what metacognition is and how it can be used to create better learners, then it is a school's job to ensure that their professional development programme addresses this. It should also not be seen as another thing that teachers need to teach but as an integrated part of their teaching where they make the implicit thinking of an experienced learner explicit.

 **Schools have a responsibility to educate their teachers on the use of metacognitive strategies if teachers don't already have a deep professional understanding of this.**

# TEACHER 2.0

Now that we have looked into the research behind metacognition, let's take a look at some practical ways in which you can act on the researchers' recommendations to enable your students to think and learn more effectively.

 ## IDEA 37: THINKING OUT LOUD

### *Let me tell you what I'm thinking right now.*

At the heart of the research behind metacognition is the fact that we don't let our students into our minds often enough every lesson. Some of the things we take for granted as an experienced learner and education professional are not second nature to our students. Even the simplest and most basic decisions that we take when planning how to solve a problem can be major barriers to learning if our students have not thought about them. By taking the time to model our thinking out loud to our students, we can begin to let them 'under the hood' of our complex and dynamic decision-making.

Although this sounds like a very simple process, in practice it can be a lot more complicated than you first think. Something called 'the curse of knowledge' can make this very difficult. This is where the more you know about something, or the more experienced you are at something, the harder it is to explain it to a novice learner. We therefore need to break our thinking and decision-making down into the smallest of steps, starting right from the beginning and describing everything you see, think and do. However, don't just do this every now and again as a separate strategy; try to integrate it into all of your modelling strategies so that it becomes a regular and subconscious daily feature of your teaching.

# IDEA 38: VISUALISER

### Let me show you what I'm thinking.

One of the most effective ways of using digital technology in the classroom over the past ten years has been with the use of a desktop visualiser. A visualiser is a small table-top camera that lets the teacher demonstrate a concept on the interactive whiteboard, by live-streaming their hand as they write out an exam answer or solve a challenging equation. The beauty of a visualiser is that students don't need to crowd around a desk to look at the process that the teacher is modelling. Instead, they can see and hear the decision-making process taking place from the comfort of their own seat.

The major benefit of this is that the decision-making and thinking are also taking place live. We've all seen the Blue Peter process ('Here's one I made earlier…'), but this loses all visibility of the metacognitive processes that we now know are so important in learning. Students don't need to see what you did earlier; they need to see you actually do it and understand the thoughts and reflections that you go through along the way. Just remember that, although they are seeing you answer the question or solve the task via the visualiser, the most important thing is that they can hear you verbalising your thinking at the same time.

# IDEA 39: WALKING TALKING MOCKS

*Let's go through this paper together.*

Taking the previous idea one step further, walking talking mocks are perfect for combining metacognitive thinking with examination skills, something that we found was missing in the Teacher 1.0 repertoire. In this strategy you set up the visualiser and hand out an exam paper to every student including yourself. Once you are set up with your exam paper, together with your hand and pen poised in front of your visualiser, you need to ensure that all of your students are also ready with their papers open at the same question. You then explicitly verbalise and visualise your thinking for each question, talking through your exact thoughts about what the question is asking you to do, how you are going to start it and what methods or techniques you are going to use. Once you have talked a question through, the students then have a specific amount of time to answer that question using the exact same thinking.

One of the significant benefits of this method is that, if done effectively by a skilled teacher who has practised and rehearsed this approach, it can be delivered to more than one class at a time. The student-to-teacher ratio is irrelevant as long as they can hear the teacher. Therefore, two, three or four classes could easily be put together in a large space (such as the main hall) and take part in this activity together to get the maximum impact from it. This also lets one of your teachers practise this approach and become skilled at it. Some teachers might shy away from talking through their every thought to 100-plus students, but with this strategy you only need one teacher to take the lead. The other teachers can wander the hall and provide expert supervision and help where required.

# IDEA 40: EXAM WRAPPERS

*Let's take a few minutes to reflect on your approach to this exam.*

After students have completed an exam, you have marked it and you are about to give them their feedback, there is a crucial stage in the metacognitive process that we usually miss out – getting students to reflect on how they have prepared for the exam without the influence of seeing their final scores or grades. Usually students with high scores will tell you that they've obviously prepared pretty well, but this might not always be the case. With an exam wrapper, students receive a series of questions about how they feel they have prepared, how many hours they have put into their revision and, more importantly, which independent study strategies they have used to revise. Depending on the specific design of the exam wrapper, students may also be asked about specific topics from the exam and requested to rate their confidence levels based on their answers.

Once this process has taken place, students then receive their completed exam papers back and are asked to look through the paper in silence, taking note of the comments and marks relating to each individual question. By cross-referencing their own thoughts and answers that they entered into the exam wrapper with their performance on the exam, they can be very self-reflective on how their preparation has influenced their performance. Once this has been completed, teachers should collect the exam wrappers for two reasons. Firstly, it lets the teacher see how each student has prepared and the correlation between preparation and performance. Secondly, those specific exam wrappers can be used again before the next exam. At the time when you want your students to start revising for their next exam, hand out their previous exam wrappers so that students can see the strengths and weaknesses of their previous approaches to revision.

**TEACHING TIP**

*In order to get an accurate picture on an exam wrapper, you need to stress the importance of being truthful. However, the only way you will achieve this is if you sell the 'why' behind this activity and make it low stakes. Even though you will be collecting them in, you need to stress that you are not marking the wrappers and they will not have any influence on scores or grades. This is simply a window into their thinking and preparation before an exam or assessment. If students aren't truthful with their answers, then the exercise is a complete waste of everyone's time.*

# FURTHER READING

If you want to continue your reading around metacognition and how it can be used to improve your students' ability to be self-reflective and self-regulative, here are some useful starting points.

▶ **Researchers:** David Perkins, Alex Quigley, Daniel Muijs, Eleanor Stringer.

▶ **Publications:** David Perkins (1992), *Smart Schools: Better thinking and learning for every child.* New York, NY: Simon and Schuster.

Alex Quigley, Daniel Muijs, Eleanor Stringer (2018), 'Metacognition and self-regulated learning: Guidance report'. London: Education Endowment Foundation.

Evidence Based Education (2018), 'Metacognition and self-regulated learning', Trialled and Tested podcast, https://evidencebased.education/ trialled-and-tested-metacognition-and-self-regulated-learning

John Flavell (1979), 'Metacognition and cognitive monitoring: A new area of cognitive–developmental inquiry', *American Psychologist*, 34, (10), 906–911.

▶ **Keyword search:** Metacognition; metacognitive thinking; metacurriculum; self-regulation; self-reflection; visualiser; exam wrapper.

# PERSONAL REFLECTION

Reflecting on this chapter, how much time and effort have you placed on developing students' metacognitive thinking skills? Has this been sufficient? And if so, what has been the impact?

Can you see ways in which you think metacognitively in your own life away from school? What are these? And how can this same thinking be applied to the classroom?

Having now read and understood the research on metacognition, how will you incorporate the research, recommendations and ideas into your daily classroom practice?

# REFERENCES

Birnbaum, M. S., Kornell, N., Bjork, E. L. and Bjork, R. A. (2013), 'Why interleaving enhances inductive learning: The roles of discrimination and retrieval', *Memory and Cognition*, 41, (3), 392–402.

Bjork, E. L. and Bjork, R. A. (2014), 'Making things hard on yourself, but in a good way: Creating desirable difficulties to enhance learning', in M. A. Gernsbacher and J. Pomerantz (eds.), *Psychology and the Real World: Essays illustrating fundamental contributions to society* (2nd edn.), (pp. 59–68). New York, NY: Worth.

Bjork, R. A. (1975), 'Retrieval as a memory modifier: An interpretation of negative recency and related phenomena', in Robert L. Solso (ed.), *Information Processing and Cognition: The Loyola Symposium*, pp. 123–144. New York, NY: Lawrence Erlbaum.

Black, P. and Wiliam, D. (1998), 'Inside the black box: Raising standards through classroom assessment', *Phi Delta Kappan*, 80, (2), 139–144.

Booth, N. (2017), 'What is formative assessment, why hasn't it worked in schools, and how can we make it better in the classroom?', *Impact*, (1).

Caviglioli, O. (2018), 'Six ways visuals help learning', *Impact*, (2).

Caviglioli, O. (2019), *Dual Coding with Teachers*. Woodbridge: John Catt.

Christodoulou, D. (2017), *Making Good Progress? The future of assessment for learning*. Oxford: Oxford University Press.

Clark, R. C. and and Lyons, C. (2010), *Graphics for Learning: Proven guidelines for planning, designing, and evaluating visuals in training materials* (2nd edn.). San Francisco, CA: Wiley.

Coe, R. (2020), 'Does research on retrieval practice translate into classroom practice?', *Impact*, (8).

Coe, R. and Kime, S. (2019), 'A (new) manifesto for evidence-based education: twenty years on'. Sunderland: Evidence Based Education.

Ebbinghaus, H. (1885), *Memory: A contribution to experimental psychology*. New York, NY: Teachers College, Columbia University.

Education Endowment Foundation (2012), 'Teaching and learning toolkit', https://educationendowmentfoundation.org.uk/evidence-summaries/teaching-learning-toolkit/

Eglington, L. G., Kang, S. H. K. (2017), 'Interleaved presentation benefits science category learning', *Journal of Applied Research in Memory and Cognition*, 6, (4), 475–485.

Evidence Based Education (2018), Metacognition and self-regulated learning', Trialled and Tested podcast https://evidencebased.education/trialled-and-tested-metacognition-and-self-regulated-learning/

Firth, J. (2018), 'The application of spacing and interleaving approaches in the classroom', *Impact*, (2).

Flavell, J. (1979), 'Metacognition and cognitive monitoring: A new area of cognitive–developmental inquiry', *American Psychologist*, 34, (10), 906–911.

Gathercole, S. and Alloway, T. P. (2007), *Understanding Working Memory, A Classroom Guide* (2nd edn.). London: Sage.

Goldacre, B. (2013), 'Building evidence into education', www.gov.uk/government/news/building-evidence-into-education

Hattie, J. (2018), *Visible Learning: Feedback*. Abingdon: Routledge.

Hendrick, C. and Macpherson, R. (2017), *What Does This Look Like in the Classroom?* Woodbridge: John Catt.

Kang, S. H. K. and Pashler, H. (2012), 'Learning painting styles: Spacing is advantageous when it promotes discriminative contrast', *Applied Cognitive Psychology*, 26, (1), 97–103.

Kohn, A. (2011), 'The case against grades', *Counterpoints*, 451, 143–153.

Kornell, N. and Bjork, R. A. (2008), 'Learning concepts and categories: Is spacing the "enemy of induction"?', *Psychological Science*, 19, (6), 585–92.

Kornell, N., Hays, M. J. and Bjork, R. A. (2009), 'Unsuccessful retrieval attempts enhance subsequent learning', *Journal of Experimental Psychology: Learning, Memory, and Cognition*, 35, (4), 989–998.

Mitchell, T. M., Shinkareva, S. V., Carlson, A., Chang, K. M., Malave, V. L., Mason, R. A. and Just, M. A. (2008), 'Predicting human brain activity associated with the meanings of nouns', *Science*, 320, (5880), 1191–1195.

National Education Union (2019), 'The state of education: workload', https://neu.org.uk/press-releases/state-education-workload

Paas, F., Renkl, A. and Sweller, J. (2003), 'Cognitive load theory and instructional design: Recent developments', *Educational Psychologist*, 38, (1), 1–4.

Paivio, A. (1986), *Mental Representations: A dual coding approach.* Oxford: Oxford University Press.

Perkins, D. (1992), *Smart Schools: Better thinking and learning for every child.* New York, NY: Simon and Schuster.

Quigley, A., Muijs, D. and Stringer, E. (2018), 'Metacognition and self-regulated learning: Guidance report'. London: Education Endowment Foundation.

Ritchhart, R. and Perkins, D. (2008), 'Making thinking visible', *Educational Leadership*, 65, (5), 57–61.

Roediger, H. L. and Karpicke, J. D. (2006), 'Test-enhanced learning: Taking memory tests improves long-term retention', *Psychological Science*, 17, (3), 249–255.

Rohrer, D. (2012), 'Interleaving helps students distinguish among similar concepts', *Educational Psychology Review*, 24, 355–367.

Rowe, M. B. (1986), 'Wait time: Slowing down may be a way of speeding up!', *Journal of Teacher Education*, 37, (1), 43–50.

Schmidt, R. A. and Lee, T. D. (2011), *Motor Control and Learning: A behavioural analysis* (5th edn.). Leeds: Human Kinetics.

Shibli, D. and West, R. (2018), , 'Cognitive load theory and its application in the classroom', *Impact*, (2).

Soderstrom, N. C. (2019), 'Learning vs. performance: A distinction every educator should know', https://medium.com/age-of-awareness/learning-vs-performance-a-distinction-every-educator-should-know-aa165a83a4f9

Soderstrom, N. C. and Bjork, R. A. (2015), 'Learning versus performance: An integrative review', *Perspectives on Psychological Science*, 10, (2), 176–199.

Stahl, R. J. (1994), 'Using "Think-Time" and "Wait-Time" skilfully in the classroom', *ERIC Digest*, ED370885.

Sumeraki, M. and Weinstein, Y. (2018), 'Optimising learning using retrieval practice', *Impact*, (2).

Sweller, J. (1988), 'Cognitive load during problem solving: Effects on learning', *Cognitive Science*, 12, (2), 257–285.

Wahlheim, C. N., Dunlosky, J. and Jacoby, L. L. (2011), 'Spacing enhances the learning of natural concepts: An investigation of mechanisms, metacognition, and aging', *Memory and Cognition*, 39, (5), 750–763.

Wiliam, D. (2009), 'Assessment for learning: Why, what and how? An inaugural professorial lecture'. London: UCL IOE Press.

Wiliam, D. (2011), *Embedded Formative Assessment*. Bloomington, IN: Solution Tree Press.

Wiliam, D. (2015), 'The research delusion', *TES*, https://www.tes.com/news/research-delusion-0

Wiliam, D. (2016), 'Dylan Wiliam – author, researcher, trainer and assessment for learning expert', Interview for Mr Barton Maths Podcast, www.mrbartonmaths.com/blog/dylan-wiliam-author-researcher-trainer-and-assessment-for-learning-expert

Wiliam, D. (2017a), *The Handbook for Embedded Formative Assessment*. Bloomington, IN: Solution Tree Press.

Wiliam, D. (2017b), 'I've come to the conclusion Sweller's Cognitive Load Theory is the single most important thing for teachers to know', Tweet, 26 January, https://twitter.com/dylanwiliam/status/824682504602943489

Wiliam, D. and Leahy, S. (2015), *Embedding Formative Assessment*. West Palm Beach, FL: Learning Sciences International.

# INDEX